MW01247004

# DODD, MEAD WONDERS BOOKS

WONDERS OF ALLIGATORS AND CROCODILES by Wyatt Blassingame
WONDERS OF ANIMAL ARCHITECTURE by Sigmund A. Lavine
WONDERS OF ANIMAL NURSERIES by Jacquelyn Berrill
WONDERS OF BARNACLES by Arnold Ross and William K. Emerson
WONDERS OF THE BAT WORLD by Sigmund A. Lavine
WONDERS BEYOND THE SOLAR SYSTEM by Rocco Feravolo
WONDERS OF THE BISON WORLD by Sigmund A. Lavine and Vincent Scuro
WONDERS OF THE CACTUS WORLD by Sigmund A. Lavine
WONDERS OF CARIBOU by Jim Rearden
WONDERS OF THE DINOSAUR WORLD by William H. Matthews III
WONDERS OF THE EAGLE WORLD by Sigmund A. Lavine
WONDERS OF THE FLY WORLD by Sigmund A. Lavine
WONDERS OF FROGS AND TOADS by Wyatt Blassingame
WONDERS OF GEESE AND SWANS by Thomas D. Fegely
WONDERS OF GEMS by Richard M. Pearl
WONDERS OF GRAVITY by Rocco Feravolo
WONDERS OF THE HAWK WORLD by Sigmund A. Lavine
WONDERS OF HERBS by Sigmund A. Lavine
WONDERS OF HUMMINGBIRDS by Hilda Simon
WONDERS OF THE KELP FOREST by Joseph E. Brown
WONDERS OF LLAMAS by Roger Perry
WONDERS OF LIONS by George and Kay Schaller
WONDERS OF MATHEMATICS by Rocco Feravolo
WONDERS OF MEASUREMENT by Owen S. Lieberg
WONDERS OF THE MONKEY WORLD by Jacquelyn Berrill
WONDERS OF THE MOSQUITO WORLD by Phil Ault
WONDERS OF THE OWL WORLD by Sigmund A. Lavine
WONDERS OF THE PELICAN WORLD by Joseph J. Cook and Ralph W. Schreiber
WONDERS OF PRAIRIE DOGS by G. Earl Chace
WONDERS OF THE PRONGHORN by G. Earl Chace
WONDERS OF RACCOONS by Wyatt Blassingame
WONDERS OF ROCKS AND MINERALS by Richard M. Pearl
WONDERS OF SAND by Christie McFall
WONDERS OF SEA GULLS by Elizabeth Anne and Ralph W. Schreiber
WONDERS OF SEALS AND SEA LIONS by Joseph E. Brown
WONDERS OF SOUND by Rocco Feravolo
WONDERS OF THE SPIDER WORLD by Sigmund A. Lavine
WONDERS OF SPONGES by Morris K. Jacobson and Rosemary K. Pang
WONDERS OF STARFISH by Morris K. Jacobson and William K. Emerson
WONDERS OF STONES by Christie McFall
WONDERS OF TERRARIUMS by Sigmund A. Lavine
WONDERS OF THE TREE WORLD by Margaret Cosgrove
WONDERS OF THE TURTLE WORLD by Wyatt Blassingame
WONDERS OF WILD DUCKS by Thomas D. Fegely
WONDERS OF THE WOODS AND DESERT AT NIGHT by Jacquelyn Berrill
WONDERS OF THE WORLD OF THE ALBATROSS by Harvey and Mildred Fisher
WONDERS OF THE WORLD OF BEARS by Bernadine Bailey
WONDERS OF THE WORLD OF HORSES by Sigmund A. Lavine and Brigid Casey
WONDERS OF THE WORLD OF SHELLS by Morris K. Jacobson and
    William K. Emerson
WONDERS OF THE WORLD OF WOLVES by Jacquelyn Berrill
WONDERS OF YOUR SENSES by Margaret Cosgrove

# Wonders of Terrariums

SIGMUND A. LAVINE

*Illustrated with photographs and with*
*line drawings by Jane O'Regan*

DODD, MEAD & COMPANY · NEW YORK

For Lisa
who always has the time

PHOTOGRAPHS AND DRAWINGS COURTESY OF:

Arnold Arboretum of Harvard University, 11, 12; Bernard Industries Co., Chicago, Illinois, 22 *bottom*, 24; Christen, Inc., St. Louis, Missouri, 6 *top and right*; Down's Collectors' Showcase, Evanston, Illinois, 23; Duro-lite Lamps, Inc., Fair Lawn, New Jersey, 25, 26; Featherock, Inc., Burbank, California, 49; Peter Paul Nurseries, Canandaigua, New York, 69; Terrestrial Terrariums, Franklin, Wisconsin, 29; Vaughan-Jacklin Company, Downer's Grove, Illinois, 75 *left*. All other photographs and drawings by Jane O'Regan.

1   2   3   4   5   6   7   8   9   10


Library of Congress Cataloging in Publication Data

Lavine, Sigmund A
    Wonders of terrariums.

    1. Glass gardens—Juvenile literature.
2. Terrariums—Juvenile literature.   I. Title.
SB417.L38        635.9′8        77-6493
ISBN 0-396-07488-X

# Contents

1. THE HISTORY OF TERRARIUMS    7
How a Terrarium Functions   7
The First Terrariums   10

2. TERRARIUM MAKING    16
Containers   16
    *Tank-type Terrariums*
    *Brandy Snifters*
    *Fishbowls*
    *Jars*
    *Bottles*
    *Domes*
Do's and Don't's   24
Lighting a Terrarium   25

3. TERRARIUM PLANTS    28
Basic Terrariums   28
Foliage or Flowers   29
    *Plants with Bright or*
      *Multicolored Foliage*
    *Flowering Plants*

4. PLANTING TECHNIQUES    40
Gathering Materials   40
    *Tools*
    *Soil*
    *Gravel*
    *Moss*
Plant Placement   47
Landscaping   49
Tank Terrariums   50
Bottles and Jugs   57

Multigallon Jugs   58
Narrow-necked Containers   59
Miniature Glass Gardens   62
Living Mobiles   63

5. TERRARIUM MAINTENANCE    65
Too Wet—Too Dry   65
More Light—Less Light   66
Too Acid—Too Alkaline   68
Pruning   69
Insects   70
Mold   71
The Last Resort   72

6. THE VERSATILE TERRARIUM    74
"The Babysitter"   74
First Aid   74
Starting Seeds   75
Propagating Plants   76
Softwood Cuttings   77
Forcing Twigs   79
Dried Arrangements   80
Holiday Terrariums   82
Growing Food   83

7. TERRARIUM ZOOS    85
Desert in a Tank   87
Woodland Terrariums   90
Marsh Terrariums   93

8. VARIATIONS ON A THEME    95

    INDEX    96

Commercial containers for terrariums come in various shapes. These four, above and to the right, have adjustable vents to control humidity. *Bottom left:* A ripple peperomia.

# 1
# *The History of Terrariums*

*"Everything has a beginning."*

Any transparent, covered container in which plants are grown is called a terrarium. Made either of plastic or glass, terrariums range in size from tiny bottles to large cases equipped with heating cables, fluorescent lights, and sliding glass panels that can be adjusted to control warmth and humidity. Terrariums also differ in shape. While glass containers are usually square, round, or oblong, those fashioned from plastic are molded in a wide variety of forms designed to make offices and stores more attractive and to blend with either traditional or modern household furnishings.

## HOW A TERRARIUM FUNCTIONS

Many plants are easier to raise in a terrarium than in pots. This is because terrariums provide a perfect setting for an indoor garden. For example, few plants can thrive in the dry heat of the average dwelling during the winter months. On the other hand, the lack of moisture in the air has no effect on a terrarium planting. If the container is tightly sealed, the high humidity that numerous plants require is maintained constantly. A terrarium also shields vegetation from sudden drafts. Moreover, it protects plants from excessive heat, unless the container is near a heating unit or receives too much sunlight. Fi-

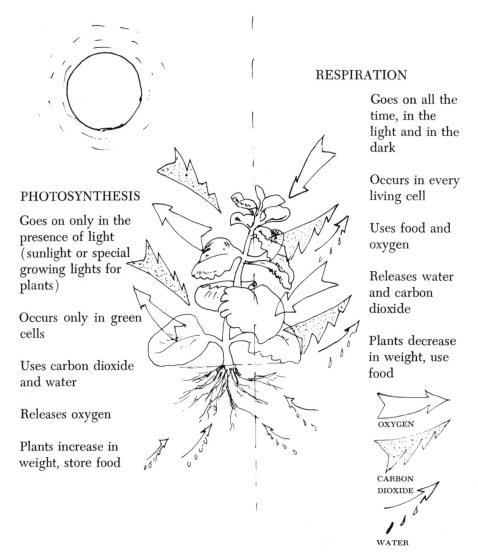

## PHOTOSYNTHESIS

Goes on only in the presence of light (sunlight or special growing lights for plants)

Occurs only in green cells

Uses carbon dioxide and water

Releases oxygen

Plants increase in weight, store food

## RESPIRATION

Goes on all the time, in the light and in the dark

Occurs in every living cell

Uses food and oxygen

Releases water and carbon dioxide

Plants decrease in weight, use food

OXYGEN

CARBON DIOXIDE

WATER

nally, a terrarium furnishes ideal conditions for the two processes that take place during the life of all plants—photosynthesis and respiration.

Botanists—students of plant life—created the word "photosynthesis." They compounded it by combining the Greek words for "light" and "putting together." Actually, few scientific words are more descriptive than photosynthesis. "Putting together by light" succinctly sums up the complicated process by which vegetation manufactures its own food. Simply stated, plants, utilizing the energy of the sun, make their food—called plant sugars—from carbon dioxide in the air and from water in the soil. While plants consume certain of these sugars as fast as they are compounded, they store others in their leaves and stems and, as they grow, convert them into food.

During respiration plants absorb oxygen from the air and "exhale" the carbon dioxide required for photosynthesis. Thus respiration and photosynthesis are interdependent. The materials created by one process make the other possible.

Photosynthesis and respiration take place at the same time. Terrarium plantings carry out both processes most efficiently,

## RAIN CYCLE

Air outside terrarium is cooler. When moist vapor rising from plants (transpiration) reaches cooler glass, it condenses, and returns to soil like rain.

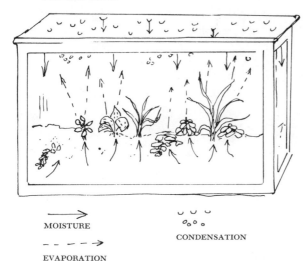

Moisture in soil is absorbed by plants and evaporated by them into the surrounding air.

→
MOISTURE

- - - →
EVAPORATION

ᵕ ᵕ ᵕ
ₒₒ ₒ
CONDENSATION

Diagram of a rain cycle: water absorbed by plant roots is released as vapor through the leaves, eventually falls to the ground, and is again absorbed by the roots in a never-ending process.

9

providing they receive sufficient moisture. Because a terrarium is a self-contained unit, water must be introduced into it. If this is not done, photosynthesis will not occur. Moistening terrarium soil not only supplies the water necessary for the manufacture of plant sugars but also establishes a rain cycle. In a rain cycle, water is absorbed by plant roots, released as vapor through the leaves, evaporates into the air, and eventually falls back into the dirt. Because the water is again absorbed by roots, a rain cycle is a never-ending process.

Once a rain cycle has been established, it provides a terrarium garden with a constant supply of moisture. Therefore a terrarium planting never has to be watered as long as condensation "fogs" the sides of the container. The tight-fitting cover not only permits the rain cycle to replenish moisture constantly but also it prevents the gases needed for photosynthesis and respiration from escaping. As a result, both processes are carried out under ideal conditions.

## THE FIRST TERRARIUMS

Although "terrarium" is derived from the Latin *terra* (earth) and *arium* (a container of), the women of ancient Greece were the first to raise plants in sealed receptacles. They sowed quick-germinating seeds or rooted seedlings in earthenware jugs during an eight-day festival held in honor of Adonis, the handsome youth beloved by Aphrodite, goddess of love. Legend holds that when Adonis was killed by a wild boar, Aphrodite was so grief stricken that the gods took pity on her. They decreed that Adonis could spend one-half of each year with Aphrodite but must remain in the underworld during the other six months. To many peoples in the ancient world, the myth detailing Adonis' death and resurrection became symbolic of the seasonal appearance and disappearance of vegetation. Thus, every spring, Greek women ceremonially mourned the dead youth, sang

10

songs asking him to return to Earth, and planted "Gardens of Adonis" which were thrown into the sea at the end of the festival.

When pagan beliefs gave way to Christianity, the ritual planting of "Gardens of Adonis" ceased. Moreover, despite the fact that Plato, the famous Greek philosopher, described the sowing of seeds in sealed containers, there is little evidence that any type of terrarium except those made in ancient Greece was constructed until early in the nineteenth century. In the summer of 1829, Nathaniel Ward, an English doctor with an insatiable curiosity about nature, made a discovery that led to the development of the modern terrarium and "brought the greenhouse into the parlor."

As a boy, Ward had pretended that he was a famous botanist while gathering plants to dry and mount. A visit to Jamaica in

One of Ward's illustrations for his book explaining "closely glazed cases." The good doctor's sense of humor is indicated by the finial on the case (a pineapple, symbol of hospitality) and the cat and mouse.

Ward's drawing of one of the cases he designed to ship plants long distances. Note how he signed this picture—his name is printed on the spine of the book.

Ward planted this terrarium and drew a picture of it about 1830. Note the base which makes this glass garden an "elegant" addition to "the drawing room."

the West Indies when he was thirteen years old not only added a number of specimens to his collection but also stimulated a desire to become an expert on tropical vegetation. However, his father did not approve and insisted that his son study medicine as he had done. In time, Ward took over his father's practice in the Whitechapel section of London but devoted his leisure time to the study of botany and gardening.

Because an old wall in Ward's backyard was unsightly, he decided to cover it with ferns and moss. But the plants withered and died. The young doctor rightly reasoned that they were affected by the smoke from nearby factories and gave up the project. Then, by a combination of luck, keen observation, and experimentation, Ward learned how to grow plants in an adverse environment.

During the summer of 1829, Ward placed damp soil and the chrysalis of a sphinx moth in a wide-mouthed bottle covered with a tin lid. While he waited for the moth to emerge, Ward was astonished to see a fern and grass sprouting from the soil. He expected the sprigs to wither, but they flourished long after

12

the moth was released. In fact, they continued to grow *unattended* for nearly four years. They would have lived even longer but the cover rusted, allowing the bottle to fill with rainwater.

Ward was convinced that the fern throve in the bottle because it was protected from the sooty factory smoke that had killed the ferns in his backyard. He also theorized that any plant that received sufficient light, warmth, and nutrients could be grown in a sealed container, providing the soil held enough moisture to maintain a rain cycle.

To test his theory, Ward placed moisture-loving ferns, desert cacti, rain-forest vegetation, and alpine plants in glass enclosures of varying sizes—including one that was eight feet square. Most of the plants prospered. For example, mosses in one of Ward's containers grew for eighteen years.

The success of his experiments prompted Ward to develop a "closely glazed" case that could be used to send plants long distances. Such a device was sorely needed. According to a spokesman for Loddiges, a nursery firm which imported thousands of plants, "only one plant in a thousand survived the voyage from China to England." There was good reason. Imported plants were shipped in ordinary packing cases aboard sailing vessels that took eight months or more to reach London from the Orient.

In June, 1833, Ward exhibited two sealed cases of living plants before the Linnean Society, an organization whose membership included England's leading botanists. The cases were then shipped to Australia. The experts who examined the plants on their arrival found them to be "in the most healthy and vigorous condition" despite the fact that they had not been watered for months and had been subjected to freezing cold and tropical heat. Moreover, plants sent back from Australia to Ward in the same cases suffered no ill effects from their long journey.

The successful shipment of plants to and from Australia along with the publication of Ward's *On the Growth of Plants in Closely Glazed Cases* led to the widespread use of portable greenhouses to transport vegetation. Known as Wardian Cases, these terrariums not only enabled botanical gardens to import successfully rare and exotic plants but also spurred a worldwide search for ornamental and commercially valuable plants.

Over the years a long list of economically important plants were carried in Wardian Cases. Chinese bananas were shipped to Fiji and Samoa, while cinchona, the plant from which quinine is derived, was transported to India in Ward's invention. When Robert Fortune was commissioned by the Honourable East India Company to secure tea plants for its plantations, he forwarded approximately twenty thousand specimens from China to the foothills of the Himalayas in the cases. After blight destroyed all the rubber trees in Ceylon, Henry Wickham, a botanist, collected thousands of seeds from wild rubber trees in Brazil, placed them in Wardian Cases, and shipped them to the Royal Botanical Gardens at Kew, England. Only two thousand of the seeds germinated but the seedlings, protected by the cases, were sent to Ceylon without the loss of a single specimen.

Wardian Cases also held the 35,000 tea plants imported by the Congress of the United States in hopes of establishing a tea industry. Although the plants arrived in excellent condition from the Orient, the project was abandoned due to the outbreak of the War Between the States.

Meanwhile, ornate Wardian cases were considered "elegant and pleasing additions to the most tasteful and elaborately furnished drawing room." Not only the wealthy enjoyed glass gardens; practically every home in England proudly displayed at least one terrarium.

Today, Dr. Ward's closely glazed container is more popular than ever. As indicated, the hot, dry air and low humidity com-

A tank-type terrarium illuminated with artificial light and set into a bookcase adds to the decor of any room. (Note the electric wire fed through hole drilled in back of bookcase.)

mon to most homes pose no problems to the gardener who grows plants inside a sealed container. If sterilized soil is used, disease-free vegetation planted, and a rain cycle established, a terrarium rarely needs attention. Not only does a sealed container do away with the chores of watering and spraying but also with the task of fertilizing. Terrarium plantings should grow slowly and the soil will supply all the nutrients they need.

Furthermore, a terrarium, while taking up far less space than a collection of potted plants, permits one to landscape on a miniature scale, thereby adding beauty to a room or hallway.

15

# 2
# Terrarium Making

*"There's a mist on the glass congealing."*

## CONTAINERS

Garden-supply centers, gift shops, florists, supermarkets, and most department stores offer a wide variety of terrarium planters. Because the majority of these containers are mass-produced they are relatively inexpensive. On the other hand, unusual cases designed to catch the eye and thus call attention to the miniature landscapes they enclose are quite costly. It is possible, however, to acquire unique planters without spending a cent. All that is required is imagination and ingenuity.

Practically any easily corked or covered glass or plastic container capable of holding enough soil to support vegetation can be converted into a "Wardian Case." Vessels made either of clear glass or plastic are best for flowering plants or vegetation with colorful foliage. The clear walls of the container not only insure sufficient light for the plants but also make them easy to see. Shade-loving vegetation can be raised in terrariums constructed of translucent materials *lightly* tinted green or amber. The plants do not make as attractive a display as those enclosed by an untinted container, but the silhouettes of plants "framed" by tinted planters make charming and unusual decorations.

16

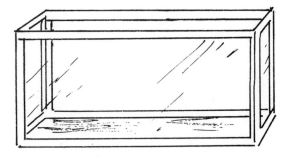

Old leaky aquariums as well as new ones make excellent containers for terrariums. They are easy to plant and maintain.

*Tank-type Terrariums*

Plexiglass cubes, fiber-glass boxes, and aquariums (including old, leaky ones) make excellent terrarium planters. Their wide openings make them ideal containers for novice glass gardeners and, when illuminated with artificial light, they can be set into bookcases, placed on shelves, or put on low tables to serve as room dividers.

Fish tanks are probably the most common oblong planters. Used aquariums are often available in secondhand stores for a fraction of their original cost. Tank containers can also be constructed inexpensively without using tools. All that is needed is window glass, masking tape, and aquarium cement. The glass and tape can be purchased in hardware stores, the cement bought wherever pet supplies are sold.

To make a tank-type terrarium, the following materials are needed:

masking tape
tube of aquarium cement
2 panes of glass 8″ × 10″ for the ends
2 panes of glass 16″ × 10″ for the sides
1 pane 16″ × 8¼″ for the base
1 pane 16″ × 8¼″ for the cover

17

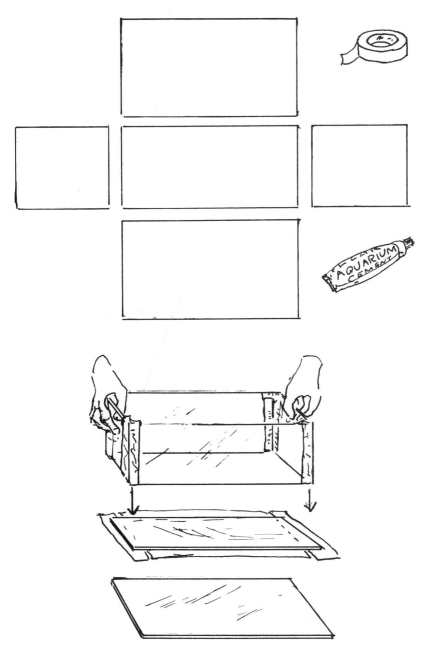

It is not difficult to make a tank terrarium with window glass, aquarium cement, and masking tape. After the cement dries, the tape is removed.

Larger or smaller tanks can be made by increasing or decreasing the dimensions of the glass.

First, cut about twenty 3- to 4-inch lengths of masking tape. Then, butt the edges of the four side pieces and tape them firmly together. Now—making sure that there are no gaps—tape the four sides to the bottom glass. Next, apply an even coat of cement along the *inside* of every seam. If any of the sealant falls on the glass, wipe it off immediately with a dry cloth. Overlooked spatters can be scraped off with a single-edge razor blade when they are thoroughly dry.

Once the tank is assembled, let it "set" for a day or two and then remove the tape that bound the pieces together. However, be sure to cover all exposed edges with masking tape. This will prevent nicking or cutting your wrists while planting.

### Brandy Snifters

Best described as oversized glasses, brandy snifters are almost as easily planted as an aquarium. As a result, florists have long used snifters to hold dish gardens. Snifters also make handsome terrariums when covered.

Ideally, a snifter should have a round cover. Any other shape detracts from its symmetry. But finding a shop willing to cut a circle out of a pane of glass or a sheet of plastic can be time-consuming. Moreover, the job is apt to be rather expensive. Both time and money can be saved by stretching plastic kitchen

An uncovered brandy snifter containing plants is a dish garden. Cover the snifter and it becomes a terrarium.

wrap over the top of a snifter. Like a glass or plastic lid, the wrap will hold humidity, maintain a rain cycle, and protect plants from changes in temperature.

### Fishbowls

Experienced fanciers rarely keep fishes in bowls. This is because, due to their shape, bowls have a much smaller water surface than tanks of the same capacity. As a result, bowls do not permit the rapid absorption of oxygen from the air. Conversely, their shape restricts the discharge of carbon dioxide exhaled by fishes. If an excess amount of carbon dioxide builds up in the water, fishes die.

However, the hand-blown "goldfish bowls" of yesteryear and more recently manufactured flat-sided fishbowls delight glass gardeners. Small fishbowls make eye-catching containers for low-growing, berry-bearing plants. Large bowls can be transformed into miniature greenhouses in which flowering deciduous twigs and clumps of violets or lily-of-the-valley can be forced.

*Above:* Fishbowls of all sizes are treasured by glass gardeners who enclose plantings by covering the bowls with plastic held in place with elastic bands. *Right:* It is time to prune or replace some of the plants in this fishbowl. They are growing too rank for the size of the container.

Few terrariums are more colorful than a fishbowl containing African violets. But although all varieties of *Saintpaulia* thrive in the high humidity of a glass garden, too much moisture will cause them to rot. This can be avoided by lifting the airtight cover on a bowl periodically. Another precaution is to place the plants so that their fuzzy leaves will not come in contact with the "rain clouds" condensed on the sides of the bowl.

*Jars*

Supermarket shelves are crammed with potential terrarium planters—the glass jars in which baby foods, jelly, mayonnaise, mustard, pickles, and other items are sold. Made of heavy glass, these jars are not particularly attractive but they have several advantages for novice terrarium gardeners. They cost nothing, have wide mouths, and are usually covered with a lid that can be screwed down tightly. Moreover, because food jars vary in

The glass jars in which various foods are sold are ideal containers for novice terrarium makers. Working with them teaches beginners the tricks and techniques of glass gardening.

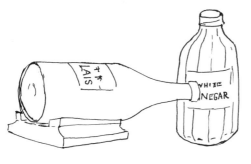

If you can insert a plant in it, any translucent or transparent bottle can be converted into a terrarium. However, it is a job that requires skill and patience.

This plastic bottle is as easy to plant as a tank terrarium—it is made in two sections.

height and diameter, working with them teaches beginners the tricks and techniques of scaling plantings to the size of a container.

*Bottles*

Any transparent or translucent bottle can be used to make a terrarium, providing you can put plants inside it. Obviously, the narrower the neck of a bottle, the more difficult it is to push vegetation through it. Actually, it is not practical for most individuals to attempt to plant inside bottles with openings smaller than a dime. However, with skill and patience, small-mouthed tiny perfume flasks, plastic medicine vials, and other such items can be turned into terrariums.

### Domes

The glass domes that once covered stuffed birds, dried flowers, and the other "keepsakes" in cluttered Victorian parlors can be used to enclose glass gardens. However, authentic nineteenth-century domes have become collectors' items and bring high prices. As a result, the average terrarium maker has to be content with relatively inexpensive, mass-produced plastic domes. Manufacturers package these reproductions with circular planters that fit snugly inside them. While there is no danger of these units breaking when hit accidentally, they do have one disadvantage—they are easily scratched.

Attractive domes can be fashioned from glass gallon or half-

A reproduction Victorian glass dome. With very little effort, it can be transformed into a charming terrarium.

Few mass-produced plastic domes are as attractive as those shaped like eggs.

gallon jugs with a bottle cutter which can be purchased in any hobby shop. Although the process is quite simple, the chances of a jug's breaking during conversion into a dome are high. Thus great care must be taken to avoid injury.

### Do's AND DON'TS

When choosing containers, bear in mind where the terrariums are to be placed. Always select a container with a design, shape, and size suitable for a given location. Otherwise, not only will glass gardens look out of place instead of adding to the attractiveness of a room but also plantings will not show to the best advantage.

Never consider setting a terrarium over a heating unit. The heat will cause the temperature inside the container to rise so high that the plants will die. The same thing will occur if a terrarium receives direct sunlight. North windows—which receive no direct sunlight—are excellent locations for terrariums. However, glass gardens can be placed on any windowsill, providing sunlight is diffused by passing through a curtain or

24

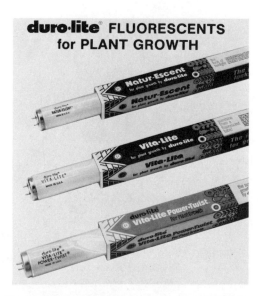

**duro·lite® FLUORESCENTS for PLANT GROWTH**

Fluorescent tubes for indoor gardening are designed to simulate natural sunshine.

slatted blind. Remember that all terrariums *must* get enough light to stimulate plant growth and to support photosynthesis.

### Lighting a terrarium

Foliage plants demand between ten to twelve hours of light daily. Flowering vegetation requires approximately sixteen hours. But frequently the only available location for a terrarium is in a dark corner of a room. In such a case, one must choose between two alternatives—to provide the terrarium with artificial light or move it near a light source every day.

Obviously, routinely carrying a terrarium from one place to another becomes a burdensome chore. It is much more practical to give a terrarium artificial light. This is best supplied by the fluorescent tubes that simulate sunlight. These tubes and the fixtures that hold them are available in electrical supply shops and large garden centers. While any fluorescent tube designed for indoor gardening will prove satisfactory, many glass gardeners have a favorite brand. The most popular are Duro-lite's Vita-Lite and Natur-Escent and Sylvania's Gro-Lux.

Besides providing illumination, plant spotlights give off beneficial heat like the sun. The higher a lamp's wattage, the greater the distance it can be from a terrarium to provide the temperature ranges for optimum growth.

Not only do fluorescents designed for indoor gardening emit the various rays plants need to grow well but also they are cool-burning. As a result, there is no danger of vegetation's drying out or of leaf scorch. Moreover, because fluorescent tubes are cheaper to operate than incandescent bulbs, it costs only pennies to burn a 20-watt tube—which will provide ample light for plants with low-light requirements—for twelve hours a day. Nor is it expensive to use a fluorescent arrangement consisting of two 40-watt tubes which will provide ample illumination for most terrarium plantings.

Both fluorescent tubes and fixtures to hold them are made in various lengths. The fixtures differ in construction. Some stand on legs while others require hanging. Still others can be placed on top of a container. The latter type is used to light aquariums and can be bought wherever tropical fish are sold. Choose the type and size fixture that best fits your terrarium and location. For example, before buying a hanging fixture, check to see if hanging it will be a difficult task and whether or not it will detract from the room's appearance.

Generally speaking, a fluorescent fixture should be placed a foot above the tops of foliage plants. If a terrarium contains flowering vegetation, the fixture should be two or three inches lower. By watching your plants, you will be able to tell whether or not they are getting the correct amount of light. If vegetation is spindly (a sign that it is reaching for light), lower the fixture. On the other hand, raise the fixture if leaves yellow slightly, indicating the container is receiving too much light.

Because incandescent bulbs generate considerable heat they are not recommended for terrarium illumination. However, "plant spotlights" (actually, specially designed incandescent bulbs) can be used to supplement natural light and to provide terrariums on a cool windowsill with heat in wintertime. These floodlights can also be used to draw attention to a glass garden or to accent a flowering or unusual plant. Because the unit containing a plant floodlight can be fastened to a wall, placed on the floor, put on a shelf, or set on a tall piece of furniture, decorator effects are created easily. *After highlighting a planting, check the temperature near the container.* If it is rising due to heat from the spotlight, move the unit farther away.

# 3
# *Terrarium Plants*

*". . . the beauty of growing plants*

As indicated, unless a glass garden is provided with artificial light, its location governs plant selection. Moreover, only species with the same light requirements should go into the same garden. Therefore, when choosing plants, one must take their individual needs for light into consideration.

Whether they prefer full sunshine or partial shade, the only plants that do well in terrariums are those species that delight in moist soil, constant temperature, and high humidity. However, rapid growth, so desirable in outdoor gardens, is out of place in a container. Slow-growing plants are better within a limited space.

Both the number of plants to be selected and their size depend upon the dimensions of the container being used. If a container is large enough to enclose several plants, the plants should differ in color, form, height, and leaf structure. Variety is as important in a terrarium as it is in an outdoor flower garden.

### BASIC TERRARIUMS

There are two basic types of glass gardens. One features vegetation and displays plants artistically. The second is a landscape which forms an entire scene in which plants are but a part.

Practically anyone can set plants in a container so that they

28

Rocks of various hues are as important to the design of this terrarium as plants. The decoration along the container's base and sides is made from colored sand.

show to best advantage. Creating landscapes not only requires imagination but also the skill to blend vegetation, natural objects such as rocks and driftwood, and manufactured articles into an harmonious whole.

The size of a container's opening is the major factor in deciding whether to plant or to landscape. Actually, with the exception of mounding soil to form hills, one can do little landscaping within the average bottle. On the other hand, the landscaping possibilities of a tank-type terrarium are almost limitless.

### FOLIAGE OR FLOWERS?

Few household decorations are more eye-catching than a glass garden ablaze with the vivid colors of certain foliage plants.

29

Similarly, a terrarium containing blossoming vegetation can be most attractive. Using flowering plants and plants with variegated leaves in the same terrarium also makes an effective display. However, it takes considerable experience in glass gardening to combine the two, and one should not attempt the task until the art of designing terrarium plantings is mastered.

Unless the right plants are chosen, no terrarium will be pleasing to the eye. To aid novices in selecting plants, the following pages list species that are easily cared for and readily available. For convenience, the recommended plants have been divided into two categories. The first list consists of foliage plants, the second of flowering vegetation.

> NOTE: *The temperature requirement of listed plants is indicated by asterisks:*
> \*     *Plants preferring cool temperatures (55°-65° F.)*
> \*\*    *Plants preferring medium temperatures (65°-75° F.)*
> \*\*\* *Plants preferring warm temperatures (75°-80° F.)*

### PLANTS WITH BRIGHT OR MULTICOLORED FOLIAGE

\*\*\* Aluminum plant (*Pilea cadierei*). Grows erect, bearing long-stalked, oval, dark-green leaves blotched with silver.

\*\* Bloodleaf (*Iresine herbstii*). The translucent red or yellow foliage of this bushy plant (which must be pruned to keep it compact) looks best in bright light.

Aluminum plant          Bloodleaf

Caladium                              Coleus

** Caladium (*Caladium bicolor*). Bearing arrow-shaped, multi-colored leaves, this tropical plant must be removed from a terrarium when its foliage dies down. After a rest, the tubers can be replanted.

** Coleus (*Coleus*). Filtered light is best for coleus, a plant whose coarsely toothed leaves are richly variegated. To keep coleus within bounds, pinch it back frequently.

** Corn plant (*Dracaena fragrans*). Although *fragrans* demands less light than other dracaenas, it grows rapidly, sending out long, swordlike leaves that resemble those of corn. Even a large terrarium may prove too small for this palmlike plant. However, a tall dracaena can be shortened by air layering. To do this, notch the stem with a sharp knife, insert a wooden toothpick in the cut to keep it open, wrap moist sphagnum moss around the wound, and cover the moss with a piece of plastic. When roots can be seen, remove the plastic and moss, sever the stem below the new roots, and pot the top of the old plant.

Corn plant—*Dracaena Sanderiana*

Croton

Devil's ivy or pothos

Certain dracaenas are much smaller than *fragrans* and grow more slowly. The best of these species for glass gardens are *Dracaena sanderiana* and *Dracaena massangeana*. *Sanderiana's* leaves are white on the margins while *massangeana's* foliage is striped with yellow. Still other small dracaenas have mottled leaves. The most popular of these is *Dracaena goldseffiana*, which is spotted with yellow. Because of its coloration, *goldseffiana* is commonly called the "gold dust plant."

** Croton (*Codiaeum variegatum*). Few plants have more handsome variegated foliage than this native of Malaya. The bronze, green, purple, red, and yellow leaves of the various species differ in structure but all are smooth and leathery.

English ivy

Ferns—*left*, tseris, *top*, Boston, and *bottom*, asparagras

\* \* Devil's ivy (*Scindapsus aureus*). Keep direct sunlight away from the coarse, blotched oval leaves of this trailing and climbing plant. *Scindapsus* is also known as pothos.

\* English ivy (*Hedera helix*). Keep direct sunlight away from this easily grown evergreen that thrives in terrariums. For color, plant one of the varieties of *helix* with spotted, striped, or variegated leaves.

\* Ferns (*Filicales*). There are six thousand species of ferns. Because the majority require a great deal of moisture, they make outstanding terrarium plants. Tropical varieties—which tolerate temperatures as high as 70° F.— can be purchased from florists, while native evergreen and deciduous ferns can be collected in moist woodlands. *Be sure and ask the landowner's permission before digging up specimens.*

33

Spurge or pachysandra

Palm—*Neanthe bella*

Peperomia

Prayer plant

Seersucker plant

*Right:* Snake plant

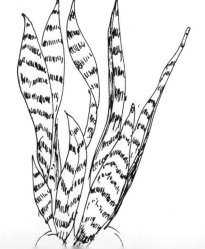

* Japanese spurge (*Pachysandra terminalis*). While there are variegated forms of this ground cover, the standard strain bears rich, dark-green rosettes of palmlike foliage.
** Palms (Aceae). *Neanthe bella*, the smallest of all palms, is ideal for terrariums because it will thrive if its roots are crowded. It has dark-green, frond-like leaves that droop in umbrella fashion.
** Peperomia (*Peperomia obtusifolia* or *Peperomia sandersii*). In a terrarium under artificial light or shaded from direct sunlight, peperomia will prosper. The different varieties will add to the attractiveness of a terrarium planting.
** Prayer plant (*Maranta leuconeura kerchoveana*). Because its large green leaves have paired brown spots, this plant is sometimes called "rabbit tracks." But prayer plant is a more appropriate common name—at night the leaves fold together, resembling hands in prayer.
** Seersucker plant (*Geogenanthus undatus*). The texture of the silver-striped leaves (which are purple underneath) gives this native of Peru its common name.
* Snake plant (*Sansevieria trifasciata*). This plant has two common names. Both stem from its long, thick leaves. Besides being known as snake plant, it is often called "mother-in-law's tongue." While all varieties of snake plant tolerate neglect and abuse, *Hahnii* is best for glass gardens. It is low growing and has vividly variegated foliage.
* Spiderwort (*Tradescantia virginiana alba*). Popularly

Spiderwort

*Left:* Strawberry begonia, which does not bear strawberries and is not a begonia! *Right:* Velvet or purple passion plant

Wandering Jew

known as the "inch plant," this shade-loving variegated creeper demands pruning. Otherwise, it will "inch" its way over an entire container.

** Strawberry begonia (*Saxifraga sarmentosa*). This is a misnamed plant, as it is not a begonia and it does not bear strawberries. But *sarmentosa* does have attractive round, fuzzy, silver-veined leaves that sprout from pinkish runners.

** Velvet plant (*Gynura aurantiaca*). A deep purple fuzz covering the spear-shaped, toothed leaves of this East Indian import gives the appearance of velvet. Because of its color, florists have given *aurantiaca* the trade name "purple passion plant."

** Wandering Jew (*Tradescantia fluminensis*). Besides *flu-*

36

*minensis,* other tradescantias are known as wandering Jew. So is *Zebrina pendula.* All these plants have thick, somewhat hairy stems and oval leaves that may be green, mauve, pink, purple, or purple-red. Because these "wanderers" are fast growers, they require frequent pruning.

FLOWERING PLANTS

* * African violet (*Saintpaulia*). Both the fuzzy foliage and colorful blossoms of African violets are attractive. Young plants of the miniature strains are best for terrariums.
 * Begonia (Begoniaceae). There are approximately one thousand species of begonias. The dwarf varieties of the fibrous-rooted type do well in a terrarium that receives filtered sunlight.
* * Cape primrose (*Streptocarpus saxorum*). This relative of African violets and gloxinias bears trumpet-shaped blossoms in pink, blue, purple, red, and white. The flowers are set off by the large, rather velvety leaves.
* * Geranium (*Pelargonium*). Standard geraniums grow too

*Left to Right:* African violet, One of the hundreds of species of begonia, Cape primrose—*Streptocarpus nexii,* Miniature Geranium

*Left to Right:* Impatiens, Lily of the valley, Miniature gloxinia

tall for glass gardens. Plant any of the midget varieties, keep them pruned, and ventilate the container to reduce the humidity.

\** Impatiens (*Impatiens sultanii*). Smaller than other members of its family, *sultanii's* bright green leaves and orange, pink, scarlet, violet, or white blossoms add color to any glass garden.

\** Lily of the valley (*Convallaria majalis*). Lily clumps dug in the fall, kept in a cool place until midwinter, and then planted in a terrarium will soon burst into bloom. Ready-to-force "pips" can also be purchased from specialists who advertise in garden magazines.

\** Miniature gloxinia (*Sinningia pusilla*). Approximately two

*Left:* Orchid—*Cypripedium acaule. Right:* Spathe

inches high, this charming plant has small, puckered, olive-green leaves that contrast with its long-tubed lavender flowers. After the blossoms fade, dig up the plant with as much dirt as possible clinging to its roots, store in a cool place for several months, then replant the tuber.

** Orchids (Orchidaceae). Several varieties of orchids can be raised in glass gardens. While most orchids require special attention, novices should have little trouble with *Cypripedium* hybrids and various wild orchids such as the lady's slipper. All do well in shaded containers. But wild orchids are protected in most states and can be poisonous to touch. Get them from a horticulturist.

* Spathe flower (*Spathiphyllum wallisii*). One of the few house plants grown for its flowers rather than for its foliage. Its blossoms resemble calla lilies in shape. Green at first, the flowers turn white, then become green again. Warning: Spathe requires strong light but dislikes direct sun.

* Violet (Violaceae). Both domesticated and wild violets thrive in cool terrariums. All violets require a great deal of water but excessive moisture causes them to rot. Therefore ventilate the container frequently.

Violets

# 4
# Planting Techniques

*"Go make thy garden. . . ."*

## GATHERING MATERIALS

Before starting the job of placing plants in a container, an experienced glass gardener makes sure he has all the materials needed to complete it. Beginners sometimes make the mistake of starting to plant as soon as they have chosen a container for a given location, selected suitable vegetation, and planned its arrangement. In their haste, novices are apt to discover that they do not have everything they need on hand. As a result, they have to stop work. This can be avoided by making a check list.

The items on this list, besides the container and all the plants, should include tools, soil, gravel, and moss if you plan to use it.

### Tools

Garden supply shops sell a great many gadgets designed for terrarium planting. Most of them are excellent. Equally efficient are children's toy gardening tools, iced-tea spoons, long-handled forks, chopsticks, icepicks, or anything else that can be used to make holes, move and arrange soil, and lift plants.

Dowels with different diameters are invaluable tools for a glass gardener. Not only is a pointed dowel the ideal device for planting in bottles but also dowels can be employed to dig holes, move rocks, and prop up plants. Fasten a cork on the end of a

PREPARED
SOIL MIX

CLEAN
GRAVEL

MOSS

WASHED
AQUARIUM
CHARCOAL

DRAINAGE
MATERIAL

Before starting to plant a container, make sure you have everything
you'll need on hand.

dowel and it becomes a soil tamper. To transform a dowel into a pruner, insert a razor blade in one end of it.

A handy gadget for planting multigallon jugs or other deep containers can be fashioned easily from a length of wire cut from a clothes hanger. If one end of the wire is bent into an open loop, it can be slipped around plant stems and used to lower vegetation into a prepared hole. The plants are then held in place with a dowel and the wire released.

It takes considerable practice to manipulate the combination of a dowel and a loop. Indeed, some individuals never master the technique. As a result, they employ one of the flexible mechanical fingers sold in hardware stores as pick-up tools. These devices are commonly called "grabbers" or tongs.

Scissors, a rubber-bulb hand sprinkler or a mister, and a watering can with a long spout are essential tools. The scissors are used to prune foliage and roots before vegetation is planted and to cut moss. A bulb sprinkler or a mister are irreplaceable for watering plantings in wide-mouthed containers. This is because their fine spray does not uproot plants. On the other hand, it is extremely difficult to water plants in bottles or other small-mouthed planters without washing them out of the soil, but a watering can with a long spout gives some control of the stream. The correct way to use a watering can is to let the water run down the sides of the container—this not only breaks the force of the water but also cleans the sides of the planter. Whenever a large amount of water is required in a specific section of a terrarium, it is best supplied with a kitchen bulb baster.

*Soil*

Unless one has access to various types of soil, it is best to use a commercial potting mix. To meet the needs of specific plants, commercial mixes are compounded in various formulas. The plants for which a particular mix is recommended are usually

42

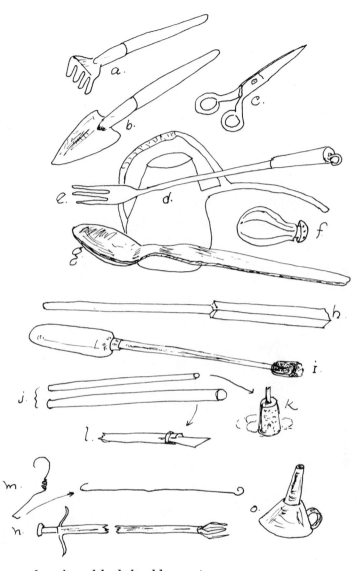

A glass gardener's toolshed should contain:
a and b. Rake and spade from child's garden set; c. Scissors; d. Long-spouted watering can; e. Long-handled fork; f. Rubber hand sprinkler; g. Long-handled spoon; h. Chopstick; i. Icepick (N.B. When not in use, always cover point with a cork); j. Dowels; k. Cork fastened to dowel for use as tamper; l. Razor blade inserted in split dowel for pruning; m. Coat hanger made into wire hook to lift and lower plants in bottles; n. "Grabber"; o. Funnel.

listed on the bag of soil. Whatever their formulas, all package mixes are guaranteed disease free, contain no weed seeds or injurious insects, and include sufficient nutrients to meet the demands of terrarium plantings.

Many terrarium makers manufacture a general-purpose mix from coarse sand, garden soil, charcoal, perlite (a form of volcanic rock), and either peat moss (dug from bogs) or leaf mold. All of these ingredients, with the exception of leaf mold, are sold in garden centers. Leaf mold—the decayed vegetation found at the base of trees—must be collected.

To make a general-purpose mix, blend equal parts of soil and peat moss or leaf mold. Next, add a half-cup each of charcoal and perlite to every two quarts of the mixture. Finally, spread the mixture on cookie sheets and bake in a 300° F. oven for half-an-hour. This sterilizes the ingredients. If you decide to make your own mix, be sure to leave a window open while it bakes— hot soil does not have the odor of a rose wet with dew!

While too much or too little soil can be put into a terrarium, all *properly* prepared glass gardens—whether tall, squat, round or square—hold proportionately the same amount of soil. This is because a container's height determines how much soil should be placed in it. The rule is: an inch of soil for each four inches of container height. However, when applying this formula, include the material used for drainage—one-eighth of an inch of gravel for every inch of soil. Thus the five inches of soil required by a planter twenty inches tall incorporate $1\frac{1}{8}$ inches of gravel.

Wide-mouthed containers can be filled either by pouring soil into them or by using a garden trowel or a large kitchen spoon. The fastest and easiest way to pour soil into bottles and other narrow-necked containers is to use a funnel. If a metal funnel is not available, a piece of heavy paper rolled into a cone can be used instead.

While various types of potting soil can be bought at garden centers, most terrarium makers prefer to mix their own and sterilize it by baking it in an oven.

EQUAL AMOUNTS OF

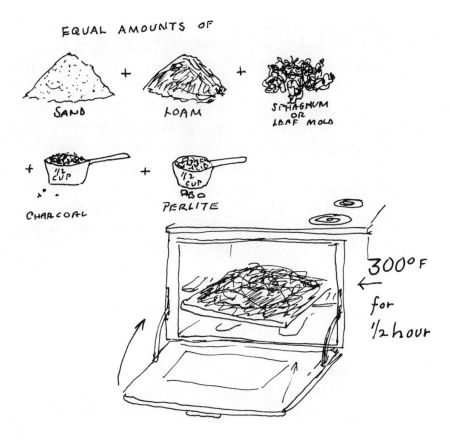

SAND + LOAM + SPHAGNUM OR LEAF MOLD

+ CHARCOAL 1/2 CUP + PERLITE 1/2 CUP ALSO

300°F for 1/2 hour

Both gravel and soil can be poured into a narrow-mouthed container with either a paper or metal funnel.

### Gravel

All terrariums contain drainage material. Otherwise the soil becomes water soaked, and the roots of plants will rot. Saturated soil also blocks out the oxygen which roots need, is suspectible to disease, and is apt to have an unpleasant odor.

Crushed rock, pebbles, pieces of broken clay pots, or aquarium gravel can be used to provide drainage in a terrarium. Aquarium gravel, sold in pet stores, is best when working in containers with narrow openings. The chore of spreading a patch of gravel as an accent or positioning a colored pebble is made easier if a piece of plastic tubing is fastened to the end of a funnel to guide the flow. Incidentally, don't try to pour wet aquarium gravel through a funnel! It will clog.

### Moss

Unless plants prefer moss rather than soil as a growing medium, lining a container really is not necessary. However, moss soaks up moisture and, as a result, prevents the lower section of a container from becoming mud stained. Either living or dried moss can be used as a lining but the living is better. A little of the green of the moss shows along the edges of the container

46

*Left:* Sphagnum moss can be purchased in garden supply centers. Before using, it should be soaked in water overnight, then squeezed damp-dry. *Right:* Look for moss for liners on rocks in damp woodlands.

most attractively. Living moss must be gathered in damp woodlands or from half-buried boulders in moist areas. If you are not lucky enough to have access to these country places, then you can buy dried moss in a plant supply store. Sphagnum moss comes dried and sterilized in plastic bags. It must be saturated, then squeezed damp-dry, before being placed in a container.

Besides being employed as a liner, moss can be spread over the drainage material to keep soil from sifting down through it. The best moss to use for this purpose is sphagnum moss.

PLANT PLACEMENT

Once a choice of plants has been made, the next step is to design the garden. If the selected plants are in pots and the container being used for the terrarium has a wide enough mouth, this is an easy task. To establish a pleasing design, merely move the pots around inside the container until their arrangement suits you. To lay out a garden in a narrow-necked

47

Positioning potted vegetation in wide-mouthed containers before planting it will help in deciding where it should be placed.

container, place the potted plants on a table and shift them about. If the plants are not separately potted, you might try sketching a few designs, to avoid moving the plants and losing the soil around their roots.

However, before switching pots from one position to another or making sketches, pick a plant to be the terrarium's focal point. Because this plant will be centrally located in the container and will tie the garden together, it should be a specimen with outstanding foliage or flowers.

After setting the focal point in place, arrange the other pots around it. To create the desired effect or to keep vegetation in proportion to a container's size, it may be necessary to prune some of the plants. Remember, plants grow, so leave gaps between them. These spaces can be filled temporarily with moss, pebbles, or bits of redwood bark.

Technically, a glass gardener should position tall background vegetation first, then work forward, establishing the focal point and placing plants along the sides and in the foreground. How-

Leave spaces between plants in a new terrarium to allow for growth.

One of the best ways to determine how to position plants in a container is to move them about on a table top.

ever, sometimes it is easier to design a complicated landscape by planting outward from the center.

### LANDSCAPING

Driftwood, bark, pebbles, or stones can be used instead of a plant as focal points in landscaped terrariums. Because large rocks can be quite heavy and there is always the danger of breaking a container when using them, it is better to make "boulders" and ledges from Featherock. Sold by garden supply shops, Featherock is a lightweight volcanic rock that can be broken into chunks, split easily, or, with very little effort, hollowed out with hammer and chisel.

Use light-weight Featherock to keep the terrarium bottom from breaking out.

*Left:* Bark is used as a focal point in this terrarium. *Right:* The little elf peering from behind the focal plant in this apple-shaped container provides a delightful accent to a simple glass garden.

While a mirror (or part of one) will produce the illusion that a landscape includes a lake, a miniature reflecting pool adds much more to a terrarium. Anything that will hold water from a bottle cap to a large bowl can be used to make a pool. Actually, rectangular vessels are as suitable for making pools as round ones—moss and stones will create an irregular "shoreline."

The realism of brooks fashioned from long, narrow plastic boxes is increased by crossing them with tiny bridges or placing miniature ceramic frogs on their banks. But birdbaths, fences, gates, sundials, toadstools, and other items designed to decorate and to provide accents for glass gardens must be used with restraint. So must animal and human figurines. Ceramic objects should blend into a landscape and not dominate it. Moreover, they must be appropriate. A lamb surrounded by tropical plants is as out of place as is a fisherman in a terrarium landscaped as a desert.

### TANK TERRARIUMS

Before setting plants in a tank terrarium, give it a thorough cleaning with hot soapy water. Then the planter must be rinsed several times to remove all trace of soap. Finally, allow the terrarium to dry. Unless its sides are completely dry, soil is apt to stick to them and may be quite difficult to remove after the plants are in place. If a glass cleaner or household ammonia must be used to eliminate stubborn stains on the glass, don't plant vegetation in it for at least three days. This will insure that all the noxious fumes from the cleaning agent have dispersed.

Don't attempt to plant a tank-type terrarium unless you are sure you have ample time to complete the job. The chances are that even if all goes smoothly it will take far longer to follow these steps than you expect.

Step 1: If you have decided not to line your terrarium with moss go to Step 2. Otherwise, either line the container with dried moss dampened and wrung out or, using a sharp scissors, cut fresh woodland moss into strips and overlap them—green side down—so that they cover the bottom of the container. Obviously, the width of the strips depends upon the size of the sheet of moss being cut. If you are lucky you may have found a boulder in a brook covered with a sheet of moss long and wide enough to enable you to make a one-piece liner.

Whether composed of dried or fresh moss, the thickness of a liner depends upon the depth of the soil that will cover it. For example, when soil slopes up from the front of a container to the

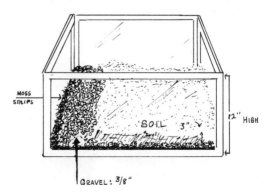

A tank container should look like this after the first three steps for converting it into a terrarium are completed.

*Left:*Spread gravel over bottom of tank or over moss liner if you have used one. *Right:* Add bits of charcoal for "sweetness."

*Left:* The first step in landscaping—creating a varying terrain. *Right:* Potted plants can be set in a tank terrarium and moved around until they create a pleasing design.

rear, the liner will vary in thickness from less than an inch to several inches in depth. Similarly, if your garden plan includes a "hill," be sure to put extra moss under it.

Step 2: Spread gravel *evenly* over the moss or unlined bottom of the container. A terrarium's terrain is created from soil, not

52

gravel. Remember, use one-eighth of an inch of gravel for every inch of soil depth.

Step 3: Cover gravel with the amount of soil required to fit the plan for your glass garden. If the soil is dry and dusty, sprinkle it lightly before placing it in the container. Dampened soil can be stored in a plastic bag.

Step 4: Plant the garden. Remove vegetation from pots with soil balls intact, set plants as deep as they stood in the pots, and tamp soil around them. When placing unpotted plants, *gently* spread their roots out and dig a hole large enough to accommodate them. This is most important! NOTE: Set fern crowns just above the soil line.

Step 5: Water plants with a hand sprayer and cover container. If tap water is used, be sure to draw it several hours ahead of time and let it stand to reach room temperature. African violets and woodland plants should be watered with rainwater if possible. Melted snow, which contains minute traces of chemicals, is beneficial to all terrarium plants.

The trick is to remove a plant from a pot with the root ball intact. To do so, support the vegetation with one hand and tap the pot's top edges.

*Left:* Background vegetation having been placed, a foreground plant is set beneath a "hill."

*Below left:* Enough water must be added to start a rain cycle, but do not drench the soil.

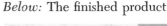

*Below:* The finished product

When watering, avoid drenching the soil. Excess water cannot evaporate in a closed container and, as a result, the soil becomes soggy and plants rot. However, enough water must be applied to start a rain cycle. If condensation does not form on the sides of the closed container, it is an indication that either more water is required or the cover of the container does not fit snugly. Gaps between cover and container can be sealed with transparent tape.

Step 6: Wipe mud or other stains off the inside walls with a lint-free cloth. A vegetable brush will remove unsightly daubs where plants have rested against the sides, while a make-up brush is ideal for cleaning dirt off foliage. A window cleaner may be used to remove fingerprints and stains from the *outside* of a container only.

Step 7: Move the terrarium to a cool, shady location for two or three days. This will help the plants adjust to their new environment.

Step 8: Place the terrarium in its permanent location. If heavy "rain clouds" condense on the sides, lift the cover and ventilate the plants.

*Left:* Rear of a newly planted terrarium. Note the dark shadow—it is water-soaked moss and soil.

*Below left:* Condensation is starting to "fog" the sides of this container.

*Below:* This terrarium needs ventilation—its sides are covered with "raindrops."

Schoolteachers making terrariums and their finished products

Before converting bottles and jugs into terrariums, they must be cleaned in the same fashion as oblong planters. While washing bottles and jugs is a relatively easy task, removing minute traces of moisture from them is a chore. Perhaps the best method of drying the inside of a bottle or jug is to direct the stream of air from an electric fan or hair dryer into the neck.

Fashioning moss liners for bottles and jugs is far more difficult than overlapping moss strips along the sides and back of an oblong planter. This is because a specific amount of moss must be used. First, make a paper pattern—a circle whose circumference is equal to the base of the container plus the number of inches of soil it requires. For example, if a bottle's base is eight inches around and its height is twelve inches, the pattern should have a circumference of eleven inches (base measurement plus one-

Because pear-shaped cookie jars have wide mouths they are not difficult to plant. They also display tall plants to advantage.

fourth of the bottle's height). It is wise to check the measurements of your paper pattern by inserting it into the planter before cutting a one-piece liner from a sheet of moss.

Before placing a one-piece liner in position, cut a number of inch-long slits along its edges. Otherwise the liner may bulge. If the opening is not big enough to admit a one-piece liner, cut the moss into sections as if slicing a pie and insert the sections individually. Remember, if living moss is used, press its green side against the bottle's bottom.

Wide-mouthed bottles and jugs are relatively easy to plant, their large openings enabling one to use a grabber or a looped wire to hold a plant in place while "shoveling" soil around its roots with a dowel.

### MULTIGALLON JUGS

The five-gallon carboys in which spring water is sold or certain chemical solutions are shipped make outstanding terrariums. The height of these jugs permits the use of tall plants and their capacity makes them easy to landscape, particularly if they have wide mouths.

No special techniques are required to convert carboys into glass gardens. The regular procedure of inserting gravel, moss, and soil into a bottle should be followed. However, multigallon jugs—like all planters that contain tall vegetation—should hold a little more soil than they require according to the soil-height formula. The extra soil not only gives added support to tall plants but also accommodates their extensive root systems. Before attempting to insert vegetation, check to see if all tools are long enough to reach the soil level. Any tool that is too short can be lengthened by fastening a dowel to it with electrician's tape.

Incidentally, an attractively planted and landscaped carboy makes a most unusual lamp. A socket for the bulb and a bracket to hold the shade can be purchased at a hardware store and

*Left:* To plant a narrow-necked carboy like this, follow the directions for narrow-necked containers. *Right:* A well-planted carboy can be made into an attractive lamp. However, to get a shade of the proper size it may be necessary to have it made to order.

mounted on a wooden stopper to fit the neck. If it is necessary to ventilate the planting, merely remove the stopper.

### NARROW-NECKED CONTAINERS

Skill and patience are required to transform bottles and jugs with narrow necks into terrariums. At times, inserting vegetation through a narrow opening and setting it in place is a tedious and frustrating job. But making a terrarium from a narrow-necked container is a challenge enthusiastic glass gardeners cannot resist. Here's how they do it.

Step 1: Cut moss for liner into segments small enough to pass through the bottle's neck. Roll segments into cylinders with the green side out (this will keep the neck clean) and push them

59

down with a dowel. Open cylinders—keep the green side down —and piece the segments together so that they overlap and rest snugly against the sides and bottom of the bottle.

Step 2: Funnel aquarium gravel into bottle and spread it over moss with a dowel. Remember, one-eighth of an inch of gravel for every inch of soil.

Step 3: Allowing for the inclusion of the gravel, pour one inch of soil into the bottle for every four inches of container height. Dry, finely sifted soil will slide quickly through a funnel; moist, coarse soil not only clogs but also is apt to smear a container's walls.

Step 4: Shake excess soil off plant roots. Usually, root balls too big to pass through a container's mouth can be compacted by *gently* rolling them on a paper towel until they become solid cylinders. If the cylinders are still larger than the diameter of the bottle's neck, the only way vegetation can be inserted is to wash all the soil off the roots.

Step 5: Make a planting hole with a pointed dowel.

Step 6: Place the roots of the focal plant into the container's neck first. Then, using a thin dowel held against the stem just above the roots, poke, push, prod, shove, thrust, and tap to make the plant slide down. Take care not to bend the foliage toward the roots while maneuvering to get the plant inside the container. If foliage bends downward, it breaks.

Step 7: Once a plant is inside the container, guide it to the hole prepared for it with a dowel. If the neck is wide enough, use two dowels, employing them like chopsticks or holding one in each hand. When the plant is in the hole, cover the roots with soil and pack the soil down firmly with a cork tamper. Roots that pop out of the soil can be anchored firmly with gravel or a pebble (but before dropping a pebble into a small-mouthed container make sure it will not become lodged in the neck). If the plant sags, prop it up with wads of moss. Bits of charcoal in

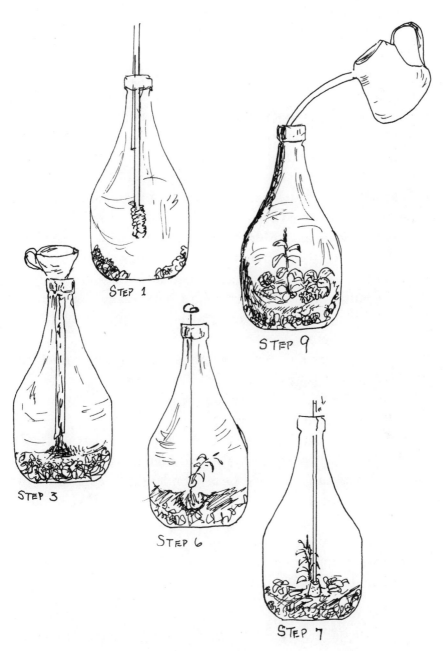

Step 1

Step 3

Step 6

Step 9

Step 7

Some of the steps in transforming a bottle into a glass garden

the moss will not only help support the plant but also will keep the terrarium "sweet."

After placing the focal plant, set the others. If, while positioning a plant, another is uprooted, stop and replant it. Otherwise, it may be injured. While working, don't hesitate to change your garden plan if it is obvious that the plants can be arranged more attractively. Just make sure that they all have room to grow.

Step 8: Water the planting with a watering can that has a long spout. If the water is directed down the sides of the container, it will, as noted, wash away any dirt clinging there. Moreover, the water will be dispersed evenly throughout the bottle or jug.

Step 9: Clean the inside of the container with a percolator brush or an oversized pipe cleaner. The latter are sold by suppliers of arts and crafts materials. Flecks of mud on the shoulders of a bottle can be removed with a pipe cleaner "mop" made by twisting several pipe cleaners together to form a half-moon and wadding their ends.

Step 10: Cover container. Before corking bottles, check the size of the cork. If, by mistake, a cork proves to be too small and falls into a bottle, don't despair. No one will ever know it is there if it is covered with moss!

Step 11: After the finished terrarium has been left in a cool, shady place for two or three days and then moved to its permanent position, watch to see if heavy condensation collects on the container's sides. If it does, it indicates that the soil is saturated. The best methods of drying out the soil are by directing the flow of air from an electric fan or a hair dryer directly into the bottle's neck or wrapping paper toweling around a dowel resting on the soil. As the towels sop up moisture, replace them with dry toweling until all the excess moisture is absorbed.

MINIATURE GLASS GARDENS

Every home does not have space for a tank-type terrarium or a glass garden in a large bottle or jug, but space can always be

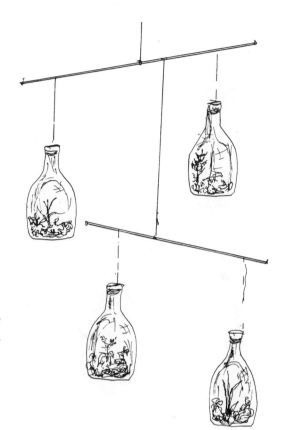

A terrarium mobile is easy to construct and makes a most unusual decoration.

found for a miniature terrarium. Lilliputian planters—such as the plastic vials in which pills are dispensed—are prepared in the same fashion as large containers. However, instead of dowels, wire loops, and a pick-up tool, the planting is done with a pencil, a bent paper clip, or a pair of tweezers. Watering a miniature terrarium is a simple matter—use an eyedropper.

### LIVING MOBILES

A mobile composed of several bottle terrariums is a true "conversation piece." First, accumulate several bottles of the same size and shape and plant ivy, philodendron, pothos, spiderwort, or baby ferns in them. Then, after a rain cycle has been established in the bottles, using fine wire suspend them individually at varying levels from crossbars hanging from the ceiling. Not only is hair wire practically invisible but also it is extremely strong. As a result, there is little danger of its snapping and causing a section of the mobile to shatter. However, when hanging the bottles, place them far enough apart so that they will not collide if they swing in a draft. And be sure they are in perfect balance by adjusting the position of the hair wires along the crossbars.

# 5
# *Terrarium Maintenance*

*"How does your garden grow?"*

Dr. Ward theorized that under ideal conditions the average plant could flourish in a terrarium for fifty years without attention. He was probably correct in his belief. However, not every terrarium is ideal. Not every one contains the proper growing medium for the vegetation planted in it, receives exactly the right amount of light, or maintains a perfect temperature. If even one of these essentials is lacking, a terrarium will not function properly. Moreover, plants die, require pruning, or grow too large for the container. Thus terrarium makers, like backyard gardeners, must keep a watchful eye on their creations. Here are some things to look for to prevent a major disaster.

## TOO WET—TOO DRY

The absence of condensation on the inside walls of a container, drooping plants, brittle foliage, dried-up moss, or parched-looking soil indicate insufficient moisture. On the other hand, extremely heavy "rain clouds" denote that the growing medium is too wet. Another sign of saturated soil—which causes plants to rot—is decaying foliage. Incidentally, too much sunlight as well as too much water will stimulate excessive condensation.

To check the moisture level in a tank-type terrarium, feel the

Technically, terrariums never need watering. But if healthy plants protected from direct sunlight droop, they probably require a drink.

soil approximately one inch below the surface. There is no accurate method of determining whether the soil in a narrow-necked container is saturated or dry. Nevertheless, some glass gardeners claim they can tell when a terrarium with a small opening requires watering by testing its weight. If the container seems light, they add water with a hand sprinkler or a long-spouted watering can.

### More light—less light

Many novice glass gardeners are apt to forget that the amount of natural light a terrarium receives varies with the season. As a result, in any given location, vegetation may get too much sunlight at times and not enough at others. If the leaves of foliage plants become "burnt" or turn yellow, the plants are probably being exposed to too much sunlight. Conversely, insufficient light may retard the blossoming of flowering vegetation.

Whenever a terrarium planting shows signs of receiving too much light it should be moved immediately to a more shady location or sheltered from the direct rays of the sun or the heat of a spotlight. If the sun that falls on a glass garden becomes less

66

intense during the winter months, the garden should be moved to a sunnier location or provided with artificial lighting.

Terrarium vegetation—except plants under evenly distributed overhead light—has a tendency to lean toward the light. Called tropism by botanists, this twisting is due to the swelling of cells on the side of the plant not exposed to light. Tropism can be counteracted by giving cylindrical containers an occasional half turn and by turning oblong containers completely around whenever the plants begin to lean. They will straighten in a day or two and the container can be returned to its original position.

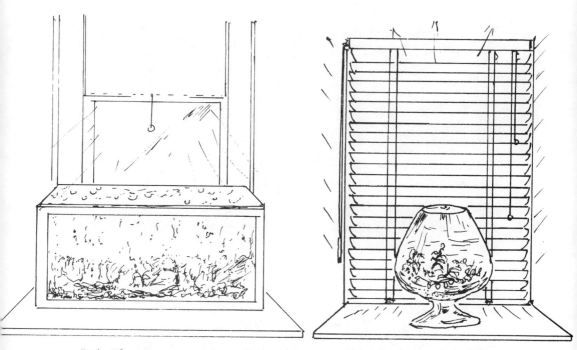

*Left:* Placing a terrarium in direct sunlight will stimulate excessive condensation and cause plantings to rot. *Right:* Drawing curtains or diffusing sunlight with a slatted blind will prevent a terrarium from receiving too much light. However, plantings must get enough light to support photosynthesis.

Plants have a tendency to lean toward the sun. Called tropism, this can be counteracted by occasionally turning containers around.

TROPISM

### Too acid—too alkaline

If plants make little or no growth, the chances are that they were placed in the wrong type of soil. Drooping alkaline-preferring vegetation will respond to a handful of agricultural lime scratched into acid soil with a dowel. Similarly, acid-loving plants will perk up if peat moss is worked into alkaline soil. But changing the composition of soil in a planted container should never be necessary. As indicated, experienced gardeners routinely check the soil requirements of specific vegetation before planting it.

Besides retarding growth, unsuitable soil is responsible for the yellowing of leaves. But don't rush to dismantle a terrarium and refill it with new soil if foliage turns yellow. The yellowing may be due to either excess light or insufficient air. Both these conditions are easily corrected. If the terrarium is receiving too much light, move it; if more air is needed, ventilate. If you are sure that the proper type of soil was used and have eliminated excess light and lack of ventilation as possible causes of leaf-yellowing, your garden is probably suffering from poor drainage —usually detected by moldy soil or a musty smell. The only way to overcome poor drainage is to dig up the plants, empty the container, and create a new glass garden.

### PRUNING

No farmer or backyard gardener ever complains that his soil is too rich. But the ideal soil for a glass garden contains only enough nutrients to insure slow, steady growth. This is because too fertile soil in a glass garden causes vegetation to grow so rapidly that it destroys the design of a planting or outgrows the container. Thus lush, rampant plants must be checked by pruning their oversized branches and excess foliage. Pruning not only keeps terrarium vegetation small but also shapes it so that it is more attractive. Even when a plant is well formed and its size is in perfect proportion to the container, it will detract from

Plant has grown too rank for this container.

a terrarium's beauty if its blossoms have faded or a leaf is dead or yellow. Both spent flowers and unsightly foliage should be removed.

Trailing plants such as ivies and tradescantias can be kept within bounds by shearing off unwanted growth. The spread of strawberry begonias and other plants that send out runners can be controlled by the selective snipping of the offshoots.

While pruning will control spreading plants, cutting the tops off most plants that have grown too tall for a container is apt to kill them. Thus when a plant outgrows a terrarium it should be removed. However, cutting the tops off tall coleus and impatiens stimulates new growth along the main stem. Similarly, pruning a fern by slicing some of the outside fronds (leaves) below the soil line with a single-edged razor blade inserted in a dowel will spur additional new, low growth. The best way of all to trim a fern is to remove it from the container and separate it into several small plants. Incidentally, if you attempt to trim a fern by cutting away the outside fronds, do the job at intervals to avoid injuring the plant.

Faded blossoms, side shoots that destroy the appearance of a landscape, and dead leaves and stems can be cut off vegetation growing in a tank-type terrarium with a small pair of scissors. To trim plants in a wide-mouthed container, hold them with a grabber and cut away rampant growth or unsightly foliage with a dowel-and-razor-blade "pruning shears." The pruned material can be removed with tongs. Because it is very difficult and often impossible to trim vegetation in narrow-necked containers it is better to reconstruct the entire planting.

### INSECTS

Because terrarium plantings are enclosed they are well protected from insect infestation *if* they were sprayed with a house-plant insecticide before being placed in the container. However, harmful pests are often concealed in root balls, while moss frequently hides the eggs of destructive species. As a matter of fact, moss collected in the woods for liners is almost certain to contain the eggs of a swarm of insects ranging from tiny sand fleas to large grasshoppers. Usually, these eggs hatch. While certain of the insects that emerge are harmless, others are capable of devastating a glass garden.

Although watching the antics of newly hatched insects is a fascinating activity, it is one no terrarium maker can afford. The young of vegetation-eating species have voracious appetites. Therefore it does not pay to take chances. As soon as any insect is seen, the plant should be sprayed with a general-purpose insecticide. Garden centers offer a number of these sprays. Be sure to follow the directions given for the one you purchase, avoid overspraying plants, and remove all traces of spray from the inside walls as soon as possible. The walls of narrow-necked containers can be dried with a lint-free cloth attached to a dowel by a rubber band. Placing pieces of paper against the sides of a large container will prevent any spray from adhering to them. After spraying, leave a container's cover off to allow all traces of the insecticides and its fumes to evaporate.

Prompt application of a spray will usually clear a terrarium of insects. However, it takes several sprayings to combat an invasion of white flies. To get rid of these hardy pests and their eggs, spray three or four times at weekly intervals. On the other hand, even a single application of insecticide is unnecessary to kill mealybugs. Actually scale insects—their popular name is due to their resemblance to flour dust—mealybugs die immediately if touched with a swab saturated with alcohol.

## MOLD

The most common disease in glass gardens is mold. This wooly growth that spreads over soil is produced by one variety of gray fungus. While its unwelcome appearance may be due to an infected plant, the usual cause of mold is too much moisture. Because the humid atmosphere in a terrarium provides mold with an ideal environment, this fungus develops very rapidly and destroys a planting within a short time.

With luck, removing an infected plant will stop the growth of mold. An infected plant should be destroyed immediately and pains taken to see that it does not come in contact with its replacement. If the new plant also falls prey to mold, dust the garden with a general-purpose fungicide which can be purchased at any garden center (be sure to follow the directions on the can). If dusting does not alleviate the situation, the terrarium must be dismantled and replanted.

### THE LAST RESORT

Unfortunately, regular maintenance of a terrarium is no guarantee that it will function properly and that the plants will flourish. As indicated, it is sometimes absolutely necessary to empty a container completely and start over again. For example, a planter's inside walls may develop a coating of green algae during the summer months. Algae is just as unattractive in a terrarium as it is in an aquarium. But while fish fanciers can destroy algae with chemicals, glass gardeners cannot. The only way they can get rid of algae is to empty the container, wash and dry it, and then refill it with fresh moss, gravel, soil, and plants.

A terrarium must also be dismantled if pruning fails to stop vegetation from growing and spoiling a carefully designed landscape. Oversized vegetation can be lifted from tank-type containers with a trowel, but it is not so easy to remove plants from a bottle with a pick-up tool or a looped wire. The best method is to uproot the plants, take hold of them near the base of their stems, and lift them roots first. This not only prevents the foliage from breaking off but also keeps the root balls more or

Unpruned, the plants have transformed a well-designed garden into a "jungle." These "baby tears" have taken over.

Few plants will withstand more neglect in a terrarium than *Sansevieria*, commonly called the snake plant.

less intact. Plants lifted in this fashion can be placed in a larger glass garden or potted for a windowsill garden. Of course, if you do not wish to save the plants, it makes no difference what method you use to remove them from a container.

# 6
# The Versatile Terrarium

*"To everything its use."*

Mastery of the art of terrarium making can be achieved only by actual experience in creating glass gardens. All a book can do is explain the various procedures used to design, plant, and maintain them. Furthermore, no book the size of this one has space to list all the ways glass and plastic containers can add to the pleasures of indoor gardening. Here you'll find only a few examples of the versatility of terrariums.

### "THE BABYSITTER"

There is no easier way to kill house plants than to take an extended vacation. Unwatered, the plants shrivel and eventually die. But house plants can be left indefinitely in a terrarium, where they will thrive unattended. If a potted plant is too tall to fit in a container it can be placed in a clear plastic bag which will function as a terrarium if the soil in which the plant is growing is saturated. Set stakes in the pot so that the plastic will not come in contact with the plant's foliage and seal the bag tightly. Plastic bag "terrariums" will supply plants with enough moisture to meet their needs for a month.

### FIRST AID

Ailing foliage and flowering vegetation often recover quickly in a terrarium "hospital." The high humidity and constant

74

temperature act as a tonic to drooping plants. Of course, the patient will not regain health if it is infected with disease, infested with insects, or planted in the wrong growing medium.

### STARTING SEEDS

Vegetable plants and flowering annuals can be raised from seed in tank-type terrariums. Sow the seeds in flats (topless boxes) or other easily drained shallow containers filled with moist, milled sphagnum moss or sterilized soil to which a liberal amount of coarse sand has been added. Tamp the growing medium before scattering the seeds. Extremely fine seeds should not be covered but should be pressed into the growing medium with the palm of the hand or a flat piece of wood.

If the flats are set on wet pebbles strewn over the bottom of the container, watering will be unnecessary until the seeds sprout. After the seedlings emerge, the flats should be watered from below by immersing them in room-temperature water. Moreover, once germination occurs, the terrarium should be uncovered during the day to provide proper ventilation. At night, replace the cover to keep the young plants warm.

Flats should not be exposed to direct sunlight. Unless they are receiving evenly distributed overhead light, flats must be turned

*Left:* Growers ship terrarium plants all year. Plants are protected by inserting pots in "flats" and placing cardboard strips in the cartons to prevent them from moving in transit. *Right:* Seedlings sprout in flats in a terrarium.

from time to time to prevent tropism. When seedlings have developed two sets of leaves, transplant them into other flats, spacing the seedlings two inches apart, or into individual pots. Although transplants can be left in a large terrarium until it is warm enough to set them outdoors, they must be uncovered. Otherwise, the plants will rot due to too much moisture.

Some glass gardeners reduce the chances of damaging seedlings during transplanting by using pellets molded from peat which expand into "pots" when moistened. They place two or three seeds in each pellet, thin seedlings to the strongest sprout, and eventually lift the pellet from the terrarium and place it where they want it. This way, there is no transplanting shock, and as the plant grows, the roots will penetrate the pellet and extend into the soil.

### PROPAGATING PLANTS

Slips taken from house plants will root readily in terrariums containing about four inches of clean, sharp sand. Don't use sand from the seashore. No matter how many times it is washed, it will retain more than enough salt crystals to kill the cuttings. Sterilized soil can also be used as a rooting medium. However, the majority of professional growers propagate cuttings either in vermiculite (derived from mica) or perlite. Both vermiculite and perlite are free of disease organisms and, in addition, do not pack tightly against cuttings as do sand and soil.

Make cuttings with a sharp knife or a single-edged razor blade. This will avoid damaging stem tissue which causes rotting. Generally speaking, it is best to cut side branches off the main stem. However, the tops of coleus, impatiens, and a few other plants can be sheared and used for cuttings.

Before inserting cuttings in a rooting medium, strip all foliage except the uppermost leaves. Buried foliage will cause cuttings to rot. Moreover, if most of the leaves are not removed,

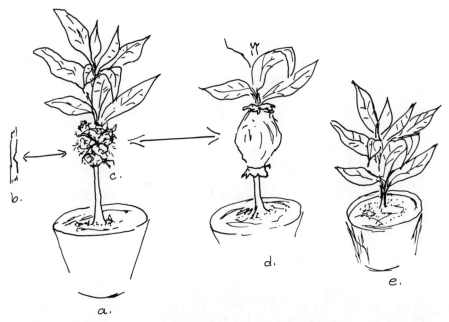

One method of propagating—air layering: a, "Leggy" plant; b, Notched cut in stem; c, Sphagnum moss secured around stem, surrounding stem and notched cut; d, Plastic secured around moss to retain moisture and promote growth of rootlets; e, Freshly rooted, now compact top of old plant newly potted.

they may demand more water than the cuttings can absorb. Place cuttings an inch deep and about two inches apart. Poking holes in the rooting medium with a pencil not only makes inserting cuttings easy but also prevents injury to their stems. Terrariums used to root house plants should be covered. However, the cover must be lifted for a short period every day to provide ventilation.

### SOFTWOOD CUTTINGS

Softwood cuttings—slips sheared from annual and perennial vegetation during the growing season—can also be propagated in terrariums. Softwood cuttings should be six inches or less in length—longer cuttings will develop into weak, spindly plants.

77

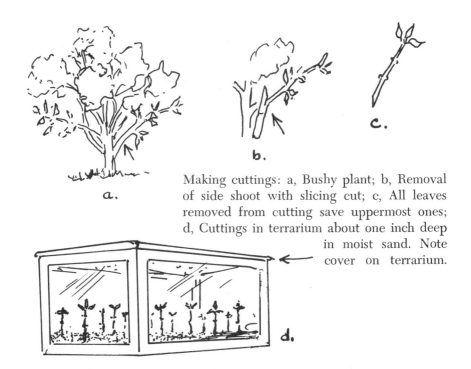

Making cuttings: a, Bushy plant; b, Removal of side shoot with slicing cut; c, All leaves removed from cutting save uppermost ones; d, Cuttings in terrarium about one inch deep in moist sand. Note cover on terrarium.

While softwood cuttings are prepared in the same manner as house-plant slips, they must be placed in a tightly sealed container which should be shaded for a week. Then the cuttings can be given dim, indirect light, and the terrarium's cover can be slightly elevated—inserting tongue depressors under it will do the trick. To determine if a cutting is ready for transplanting, carefully lift it with an old fork or a notched stick. If there are roots it will offer resistance. If no roots have formed or they are not developed enough to support the cutting, it should be put back into the rooting medium.

During root formation, water the growing medium with a hand sprinkler whenever it is dry. Once the cuttings are well-rooted, they can be transplanted into individual pots or set outdoors. If placed in the open, they should be kept moist and shaded from the sun until they are established.

78

### FORCING TWIGS

Glass gardeners can enjoy the beauty of spring during the dark cold days of winter by placing budded twigs in a terrarium and forcing them to bloom. The twigs are cut from deciduous vegetation—shrubs and trees that lose their foliage each autumn. Many deciduous species form their buds in the fall. Included in this group are alder, birch, maple, and willow, as well as fruit trees, flowering quince, forsythia, lilac, and pussy willow. All are easy to force. Branches cut in mid-winter after they have been subjected to freezing temperatures respond to the heat and warmth of a terrarium by bursting into bloom within two to six weeks.

Individuals who have shrubs in their back yards or access to a wooded lot can acquire enough of these twigs to fill a dozen terrariums. Residents of cities are not so fortunate. Unless they have a back yard or are able to acquire twigs when tree-trimmers are at work in their neighborhoods, they must take a trip and search for twigs along a country road or buy budded branches of forsythia and pussy willows from the specialists who advertise in garden magazines.

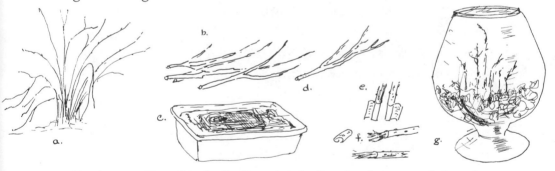

Forcing: a, Forsythia bush, January; b, Bunch of unopened forsythia twigs; c, Twigs submerged in water in dishpan, held beneath surface by block of wood; d, Twigs removed from water; e. Twigs with inch of bark removed from base; f, Peeled sections mashed; g. Twigs in terrarium containing sphagnum moss (four-fifths of an inch deep) arranged according to height. Container should be covered.

Deciduous twigs cut for forcing should be at least eight inches long. To help them adjust to being suddenly subjected to warmer temperatures, it is best to store them overnight in a cool place. The following morning, plunge them into cold water and keep them submerged for a day. This will fill their tissues with water. Finally, remove about an inch of bark from the base of each twig and pound the peeled sections with a hammer to stimulate the swelling of growth cells. The twigs can now be placed in a container.

Use either aquarium gravel or shredded sphagnum moss as a forcing medium. It takes between four and five inches of gravel or moss to hold the twigs upright. Space the twigs so that the blossoms have ample room to develop. The twigs should also be arranged in a pleasing design according to their height. Cover the container loosely—excessive humidity will cause mold to form on the buds. If mold does appear, ventilate the container by removing the cover, and when the forcing medium begins to dry out, water it with a hand sprinkler.

Success in forcing twigs depends upon reproducing spring-like conditions in a terrarium. Therefore the container must be placed where it will receive little light and the temperature averages between 50° and 70° F. After the buds begin to show color, they should be exposed to more light. Avoid direct sunlight—it will cause blossoms to fade within a short time. Experienced glass gardeners lengthen the flowering period of deciduous twigs in a small container by putting the planter in a refrigerator at night. (Incidentally, African violets raised in terrariums hold their blossoms for a longer period if treated in the same fashion.)

DRIED ARRANGEMENTS

Dr. Ward probably would not approve of terrariums containing dried arrangements. Nevertheless, they do make charming decorations. Unlike bouquets of dried vegetation in vases, they do not become covered with dust but remain fresh, colorful, and attractive because they are in sealed containers. Fields, gardens, and woodlands contain an almost unlimited supply of materials for dried arrangements. Among the easiest vegetation to work with are dried berries, everlastings, ferns, flowers, grasses (both wild and ornamental), rose haws, husks, and seed pods.

Material for dried arrangements should be cut on a sunny day after the dew has evaporated. To dry flowers, place them head down in a box filled either with borax or silica gel (sold in garden shops). Blossoms dry in silica gel in about a week; those placed in borax in approximately two weeks. Non-flowering material, everlastings, and strawflowers are best dried by tying them in bundles which are hung in a dimly lit, airy place. The process will take ten days or more.

Because dried vegetation is brittle and likely to snap while being pushed through a narrow opening, use only wide-mouthed containers for dried arrangements. Either floral clay spread over the bottom of the container with a dowel or needled flower holders secured with clay will hold the material in place. Holes punched in the clay with a piece of wire will reduce the chances of stems breaking while being set in place. Conceal the clay and holders with a layer of dried moss, lichen-covered bark, or white or colored aquarium gravel. Then seal the container tightly by applying rubber cement to its rim and the outside edges of the cover.

Dried arrangements in sealed containers will retain most of their color indefinitely unless exposed to direct sunlight. The slight fading that does occur—particularly of white flowers—softens the various hues and often makes an arrangement more attractive.

High humidity will cause dried arrangements to disintegrate. Thus it is a wise precaution to sprinkle a teaspoonful of silica

Suggested seasonal terrariums: a, Small Nativity scene with *Neanthe bella* palm, moss, and trailing plants such as ivy or species of peperomia; b, Ceramic turkey set amidst small ferns, wild cranberry, and other green plants suitable for a background. Both containers are covered.

gel over the clay or flower holders before camouflaging them with moss or bark. If this preventive measure fails and condensation fogs the container's inside walls, remove the cover and place the planter in a warm, dry location for several days.

### Holiday terrariums

No glass gardens attract more favorable comment than those designed to serve as centerpieces and room decorations on holidays. Partridgeberry bowls add to the festivity of Christmas. So do miniature terrariums created from clear, plastic Christmas tree ornaments, providing they can be cut in half with a single-edged razor blade without damage and the halves rejoined with transparent tape. Plant them in the same fashion as pill vials, perfume bottles, and other tiny containers.

With a little patience and much imagination, the plastic, heart-shaped boxes in which candy is sold in celebration of St. Valentine's Day can be converted into terrariums filled with flowering plants. Similarly, both the costly crystal eggs manufactured in Europe and the inexpensive plastic eggs in which marshmallow chicks and ducklings are packaged make perfect containers for Easter terrariums. Not only do seasonal terrariums and unusual glass gardens make unique gifts but also they sell well at garage sales and at flea markets.

### GROWING FOOD

A tank terrarium makes a most satisfactory garden for city dwellers. Some crops can actually be raised in a wide-mouthed quart jar without soil. This harvest consists of sprouted alfalfa or wheat seeds which are widely used in salads by those who include the so-called "health foods" in their diets.

To sprout alfalfa and wheat seed—both are sold in natural food stores—soak them overnight in barely enough water to

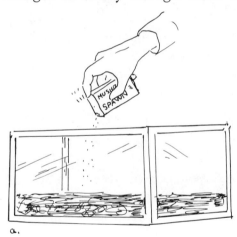

Growing food in a terrarium: a, Mushroom spawn is sprinkled over soil rich in humus in a tank; b, Tiny buttons appear. Magnified view shows detail of appearance before cap separates from stem.

cover them. Drain the water by covering the mouth of the jar with a piece of cheesecloth held in place by a rubber band. Because the seeds will compact on the bottom of the jar, turn it on its side to spread the seeds over a larger area. Rinse and drain the seeds daily in cool water until they germinate.

Once sprouts appear, give the jar more light but do not expose it to direct sunlight. When the majority of the seeds have germinated, remove the cheesecloth, screw the jar's cover on tightly, and put the jar in the refrigerator. There, the sprouts will stay fresh and green for about a week.

Nothing adds more zest to a salad than garden cress. It is easy to raise in a glass garden. Two or three flats planted at ten-day intervals will provide an abundant and continuous supply of crisp, peppery cress. Cut the plants with a scissors when they are about two inches high. After reaping two or three crops, pull up the plants and replant the flats.

Epicures—individuals who delight in fine food—often raise mushrooms in terrariums. It is not difficult. Sow mushroom spawn—available from specialists—on wet, fertile soil and keep the container where the temperature ranges between 55° and 60° F. and the light is dim.

Three weeks after the spawn is planted, the first "flush" (tiny mushrooms) will appear. The mushrooms are ready to pick when the "veil" connecting the bottom of the cap to the stem breaks. Successive flushes follow one another at three-week intervals until the fertility of the soil is exhausted. Then the top layer of soil must be replaced and more spawn scattered thinly over it.

Preplanted mushroom gardens consisting of plastic-covered trays containing spawn and soil are also available from seed houses. While both preplanted planters and spawn will yield bumper crops if conditions are favorable, neither will produce flushes in warm weather.

# 7
# Terrarium Zoos

*". . . . and beasts were there."*

Do you know what a habitat is?

Simply defined, a habitat is the locale where specific species of plants grow or animals live. For example, the habitat of wintergreen—called checkerberry by those who chew its leaves—is dry woodland where it grows in acid soil in partial shade. The habitat of the misnamed horned toad (it is actually a lizard) is the desert area of Mexico and the American Southwest.

Successful glass gardeners artificially create the proper habitat for their plantings by using the correct type of soil and meeting the heat and light requirements of the vegetation in their terrariums. Similarly, the habitats of a long list of animals ranging from insects to snakes can be duplicated in a glass or plastic container. Technically, when a terrarium houses animals, it becomes a vivarium. Irrespective of what it is called, a container zoo will provide anyone interested in the wiles and ways of nature with countless hours of enjoyment.

But a vivarium is a responsibility as well as a pleasure. Its inhabitants must be fed, their living quarters kept clean, and, in some instances, special care given to female and young. Thus, before converting a terrarium into a zoo, one should be positive that he will *never* neglect the animals it contains. Remember, if you are ill, or on vacation, someone in the family will have to act as zoo keeper. So check and make sure no one objects to having a menagerie in the house.

If there is no danger of your pets suffering from lack of attention, you can then decide the kind of terrarium zoo you want. There are three basic types: desert, woodland, and bog. Some authorities refer to the last named as a marsh-swamp-stream vivarium. The desert type should have a screen and a light.

Obviously, the pets that will live in a terrarium zoo determine which environment should be created. Other considerations include the size of the container—tank-type terrariums are best for all habitats—and the ease with which food can be acquired and fed. Supplying a turtle with chopped vegetables, fruit, lettuce leaves, and either canned dog or cat food is neither difficult nor costly. On the other hand, furnishing live frogs, lizards, or mice to a snake not only entails considerable effort but also can be quite expensive.

There are two ways to stock a vivarium. One is to patronize a pet store. The other is to collect specimens. If you decide to become a "big game hunter," ask your local museum of natural history or your library for books detailing the techniques of netting small creatures. An even better method of learning how to capture them is to accompany an experienced naturalist on a field trip. The lessons you learn will greatly reduce the chances of harming your quarries.

Meanwhile, write the conservation department of your state and request its list of rare and endangered species protected by law. You may be astonished to find that the list includes certain frogs, toads, snakes, and turtles. This means you must become familiar with the various species of the animals you wish to collect. Such knowledge will not only prevent you from breaking the law but also will keep you from mistaking a venomous snake for a harmless one.

A desert habitat is the easiest of the three basic vivariums to design, plant, and maintain. However, special care must be taken to meet the demands of the animals and plants it encloses. A container desert must be placed so its "climate" is always warm and dry. Temperatures inside the container should range between 70° to 90° F. during the day and never drop below 60° F. at night. In some locations it may be necessary to heat a desert habitat in the evening. This is best done with a light bulb shielded by an aquarium reflector. Conversely, if the container is exposed to direct sunlight, it must be shaded if the temperature rises about 90° F.

The same procedures for making an ordinary terrarium are followed when creating a desert habitat. However, after approximately two inches of soil have been spread over the tank, the

Terrariums containing cacti must be well ventilated. The plants should be kept in pots for easy handling.

soil must be covered with six inches of clean, fine sand. This thick layer of sand is a necessity—desert creatures have the habit of burying themselves to sleep at night or to keep cool during the day. Because the sand must be absolutely clean, wash it several times and then dry it thoroughly by baking or by exposure to the sun.

Cacti are the best plants for a desert habitat. Florists stock numerous inexpensive varieties which differ in shape and size. Thus, by careful selection of cacti, one can landscape the flat desert terrain. When planting cacti, leave them in their pots and bury the pots in the sand—this makes them easier to handle. Cacti spines are not only sharper than a needle but also most difficult to remove from a finger.

A ceramic burro, a miniature pick and shovel, a bit of bleached bone, or a small, crudely lettered sign indicating the trail to a mine will add interest to a desert landscape. So will weathered rock piled to form a cave. In addition to being decorative, the cave will also provide a nook in which the residents of the zoo can hide.

Numerous lizards from all parts of the world, certain harmless snakes, tarantulas, and tortoises are the most suitable animals for a desert terrarium. However, if they are to remain healthy and contented, one must know what, when, and how to feed them. This data should be acquired from books or from animal dealers *before* specimens are purchased or collected. Meanwhile, here are a few suggestions.

Among the many lizards that adapt to captivity are species that relish dog food. Others eat earthworms. A year-long supply of earthworms can be insured by placing some worms in a container filled with rotting leaves and fertile soil. Keep the container constantly moist in a cool location and work some cooked oatmeal and the yoke of a hard-boiled egg into the leaf-soil mixture every three weeks to furnish food for the worms.

A desert terrarium. There should be a screened top and an aquarium-type light to keep the reptiles warm. Dried grasses at back in corner are sprayed each morning so lizards can lick "dew." Note the removable water dish and the slabs of slate or limestone for the use of the whip-tailed lizard or racerunner on piece of dried wood and the banded gecko in the cave.

It is far more difficult to satisfy a tarantula's appetite than to feed a lizard. Like all spiders, tarantulas prey on live insects. When feeding a tarantula, merely drop its meal into the container. The tarantula will eat when it is hungry. Never try to tempt one of these hairy, ugly spiders to eat by pushing an insect toward it. The motion of your hand may startle the tarantula and provoke it to bite. Unlike venomous snakes—which should *never* be kept in a terrarium zoo—tarantulas are mild-mannered and only bite when frightened.

Tortoises should be fed once a week. Their diet includes meat, vegetables, and fruit. Tortoises also require a "water hole." This can be made easily by sinking a small bowl in the sand. Incidentally, certain desert animals quench their thirst by lapping dew off vegetation. If you acquire a specimen that drinks in this fashion, you can provide it with "dew" by placing a handful of dried grass in a corner of the terrarium and watering it daily with a hand sprinkler.

As indicated, snakes demand live food—frogs, lizards, and mice. They should be fed whenever they will eat. Generally speaking, large snakes are content with a big meal once a month; small snakes are satisfied with "light lunches" twice a week.

## Woodland terrariums

City residents may live in huge apartment buildings, two family houses, or single homes. Similarly woodland animals differ greatly in their choice of abodes. Thus, to meet the needs of various species, a woodland terrarium may duplicate a cluster of ferns and mosses near a brook, reproduce the forest floor, or simulate a pond in a glen.

While woodland terrariums are prepared like all glass gardens, an inch or two of peat moss or leaf mold should be laid on top of the soil. If you go on a leaf-mold-collecting expedition in the country, don't forget to look for low-growing plants. Club mosses, creeping snowberry, evergreen seedlings, partridge berry, and small ferns make a woodland terrarium far more realistic than anything sold by a florist. But before gathering a single plant, make sure it is not a protected species. It is equally important to ask permission of landowners to remove plants from their property.

Besides plants, a woodland habitat should include a small rock, sections of bark, and twigs. A good landscaping trick is to leave gaps between rocks and set vegetation there. If a snake is to occupy the terrarium, make a flat rock its focal point—snakes delight in curling up on a sun-baked rock.

Every woodland habitat should contain a pond. Its size will depend upon the container's capacity and the habits of the zoo's residents. For example, amphibians require a swimming hole, but the small green turtles sold in pet shops will be perfectly

90

Not only will moss, small stones, bits of bark, and dried grass hide the edges of a vessel used to make a pond but also they will create an irregular shoreline.

content with a shallow pool, providing it contains rocks on which they can climb and bask.

Conscientious zoo keepers change the water in their woodland terrarium pools at least once a day. To avoid eroding the shoreline of the pond and to prevent plants from being uprooted, most of them make a pond from two containers. The first is set permanently in place while the second, which holds the water, is laid on top of it, just as dishes are stacked on a shelf. Because only the upper dish is removed when the pond needs cleaning or filling, the landscaping is not damaged.

Many communities purify their water with chlorine, a chemical that is toxic to animals. Thus it is not advisable to fill terrarium ponds with water taken directly from the tap. Instead, let the water age by standing in a loosely covered container for thirty-six hours. It then will be chlorine-free. Plastic gallon jugs are excellent vessels for aging water as they do not break. Use two jugs as a reservoir—while the water in one is aging, utilize the contents of the other.

Woodland terrarium. Glass top is slightly raised to allow circulation of air by using split rubber tubing in short lengths. Note removable water pan and old leaves for concealment of inhabitants if they desire.

Marsh-swamp-stream terrarium. Water containers *must* be removable to keep them clean and sweet. Top is raised slightly to provide fresh air to inhabitants. All plants in such a terrarium must like an acid soil.

It would require dozens of tanks to hold all the animals that can be kept in a woodland terrarium. Among the best are frogs, lizards, newts, snakes, toads, and turtles. Because some of these creatures are natural enemies, choose only species that will live in harmony. Moreover, all the animals should be of the same size—smaller specimens may be bullied and suffer from lack of food.

Frogs and newts will eat earthworms. Newts also relish small insects and tubifex worms. The latter are used to feed tropical fish and can be purchased in pet shops. So can mealworm cultures. Actually the larvae of a beetle, mealworms are easy to raise and can be fed to frogs, toads, lizards, and some snakes. All amphibians and certain reptiles may develop a liking for canned dog food. Frogs, toads, and other amphibians should be fed at least twice a week.

## Marsh terrariums

Marsh soil is moist, fertile, and acid. Thus the ideal soil to use when constructing a marsh-swamp-stream habitat is that dug up in a bog. However, ordinary garden soil can be made acid by mixing a liberal amount of peat moss into it. Packaged synthetic acid soil can also be purchased at garden centers.

The stream in a marsh terrarium must also be acid. The only sure way to determine whether the water in your community is acid, alkaline, or neutral is to buy a water-testing kit. Available in pet stores, these inexpensive kits also include materials for changing the chemical condition of water.

No terrarium zoo is more difficult to create than the marsh-swamp-stream habitat. This is because the terrarium encloses both land and water. To separate the two, divide the container with a piece of glass set edgewise and anchor it in place with clear aquarium cement.

Slope the land section—which should be planted with small evergreen seedlings, mosses, and ferns—toward the stream. Because food and animal wastes will quickly turn the stream into a foul-smelling brew, it demands frequent cleaning. The "stacked dish" technique is the best way to make this task as simple as possible. Any aquatic vegetation in the stream should be in pots so that it too can be lifted easily.

The amount of light a marsh terrarium receives is most important. Only in the very early morning should it be exposed to direct sunlight. The rest of the day the container should get only indirect sunlight. Temperatures inside the terrarium should range from 75° to 80° F. during the day and drop to between 60° to 65° F. at night. Covering the container with a pane of glass will reduce heat loss. The pane must be raised to allow air to flow constantly in and out of the container; yet it must fit tightly enough to prevent any animal from escaping. This is best done by spreading small-meshed wire netting (available at hardware stores) over the mouth of the container and resting the glass on it. Whenever the temperature inside the terrarium becomes too warm, remove the glass.

Frogs, garter snakes, tadpoles, toads, newts, salamanders, skinks, and snails do well in a marsh-swamp-stream habitat. Both pond snails and the spotted newt will reproduce readily in captivity. The courtship rites of the spotted newt are spectacular and attempting to breed it is a worthwhile activity for any nature lover. If you are fortunate enough to have a pair of newts breed, move their eggs to another terrarium. Otherwise, when the babies hatch, their parents will eat them.

94

# 8
# *Variations on a Theme*

*"You never know what you can do till you try."*

Whether they contain a single plant or enclose a thoughtfully designed and beautifully planted landscape, all terrariums function in the same way. Nevertheless, there are countless variations of Dr. Ward's "closely glazed case." This is because creative individuals are constantly constructing unique glass gardens. To these artisans any clear or lightly tinted glass or plastic container from an antique kerosene lantern to a modern glass-topped coffee table is a potential planter.

Once you have mastered the basic skills of terrarium making, you, too, can give full rein to your inventiveness. For example, why not duplicate in miniature a favorite picnic spot or construct a bog in which insect-eating plants grow? If you try to raise cannibalistic vegetation, you must supply it with fruit flies or drop scraps of meat into its traps or onto the sticky leaves with a pair of tweezers.

Naturally, not all your projects will be successful. But you'll find few hobbies as rewarding as transforming a discarded bottle, jar, or aquarium into a thing of beauty. This is particularly true if one is not afraid to try to create something unusual. Good luck—and may all your glass gardens thrive!

# Index

Algae, 72
Animals
  collecting, 86
  for desert habitat, 88–90
  for marsh habitat, 93
  for woodland habitat, 93
Charcoal, 60
Containers, 16–24
  bottles, 22, 27, 57, 59, 60, 62
  brandy snifters, 19–20
  domes, 23–24
  fishbowls, 20–21
  jars, 21–22
  jugs, 51, 57–59
  lilliputian, 63
  making tank type, 17–19
  multigallon, 42, 58–59
  narrow-necked, 47–48, 59–60
  selection of, 24
  tank type, 17–19, 29, 50–55
Dried arrangements, 79–85
Featherock, 49
Figurines, 50, 88
Focal point, 48
Food growing, 83
Forcing twigs, 79–80
Fungicide, 72
Gravel, 46, 80
  formula for use, 53
Insects, 70–71
Landscaping, 49–50
Leaf mold, 44, 90
Light, 17, 28, 66–67, 68, 75
  artificial, 25–27
Mobiles, 63–64
Mold, 71–72
Moss, 44, 46–47, 51, 59–60
  liners, 46, 57–58
  living, 47, 48
  peat, 44
  sphagnum, 47, 75, 80
Mushroom spawn, 84
Perlite, 44
Photosynthesis, 8–10, 25
Plants, 28–39
  cacti, 88
  insect-eating, 95
  flowering, 37–39

foliage, 30–37
  placement of, 47–48
  selection of, 28–30
  wild, 90
Propagating, 76–78
Pruning, 42, 65, 69–70
Rain cycle, 9, 10, 20, 63
Respiration, 8
Sand, 44
Seeds
  starting, 75
  care of seedlings, 75–76
Soil
  acid, 68, 93
  alkaline, 68
  commercial mixes, 42, 44
  formula for use, 44
  general purpose, 44–45
  marsh, 93
Spraying, 70–71
Temperature, 65, 80, 94
Terrariums
  functioning of, 7–10
  history of, 10–13
  holiday, 82–83
  locating, 24–25
  maintenance of, 65–66, 72–75
  miniature, 62–63
  planting of, 40–64
  use in food growing, 83–84
Tools, 40–42
Transplanting, 76
Tropism, 67, 76
Ventilation, 55, 67–68, 83
Vermiculite, 76
Vivariums, 85–86
  desert habitat, 87–90
  marsh habitat, 93–94
  pools in, 90–91
  woodland habitat, 93–94
Ward, Dr. Nathaniel, 11–14, 65, 80, 95
Wardian Case, 13–14, 16
Water
  aging, 9
  necessary for photosynthesis, 10
  reflecting pools, 50
Watering, 42, 53–54, 63
Water-testing kits, 93